T5-BYG-609

THE MARKETING OF PROFESSIONAL ACCOUNTING SERVICES

JAMES J. MAHON, CPA

THE MARKETING OF PROFESSIONAL ACCOUNTING SERVICES

A RONALD PRESS PUBLICATION

JOHN WILEY & SONS
New York • Chichester • Brisbane • Toronto

Library of Congress Cataloging in Publication Data

Mahon, James Joseph, 1912–
   The marketing of professional accounting services.

   "A Wiley-Interscience publication."
   Includes index.
   1. Advertising—Accountants. 2. Marketing.
I. Title.
HF6161.A3M33   658.89′657′61   78-18221
ISBN 0-471-04480-6

Printed in United States of America

10 9 8 7 6 5 4 3 2 1

for **MONICA**

Preface

It is sheer coincidence that this book is emerging just when the accounting profession is in the process of relaxing its long-standing bans on competitive bidding, advertising, and promotional practices. For the book has been contemplated for almost twenty years and indeed some of the material was written almost that long ago—although it represents but a small part of the work.

It was around 1958 when the managing partner of our firm persuaded me to transfer from the Philadelphia office to the New York headquarters to initiate a nationwide practice development function and to assist in building an international practice. Until that time, I had been almost completely immersed in tax practice. And while I had been able to attract some new clients through extensive speaking and writing activities, it was quite another thing to articulate these abilities and transfer them to others in the firm—let alone to motivate them to undertake types of promotional activity that somehow seemed to go against their professional grain.

Unfortunately, the professional literature contained little on the marketing of professional services. I queried a number of successful accountants on how they had developed their practices. But their explanations were vague. Some replied that they had "sold, sold, sold"; others reported they "just happened to be in the right place at the right time"; and still others attributed their success to simply "performing good work"—all of which were undoubtedly true, but not very definitive. It seemed to me that developing and maintaining a large flow of new business required something more positive and structured than mere chance.

I began to evolve a development program for the firm practically from scratch. And I resolved I would some day fill the conspicuous gap in the literature on the marketing of professional accounting services. I felt that if I did not document this vital aspect of accountancy no one would. Unlike the technical areas—auditing, taxes, and management services—which have always been able to attract chroniclers, the behind-the-scenes marketing function has been relatively obscure. Few are familiar with it. But having spawned a full-fledged practice development function for a major firm in 1958, and having nurtured it for fourteen years, I now feel qualified to describe it.

I had been a close and indeed privileged observer of accountancy for many years. I was first introduced to the profession when I studied Montgomery's Auditing in the Wharton School in 1931. But through close association with such noted Pennsylvania pioneers as William Main and T. Edward Ross, I learned firsthand much about the American profession's formation and its early years (including how several of its illustrious members got home during the Blizzard of '88—they walked!). As a taxman and an outsider to the profession's mainstream, auditing, I felt particularly equipped to perceive and comment on the changes in its environment and marketplace over the years. Thus, this work on the marketing of professional accounting services.

In approaching the subject I found it impossible to separate the marketing features from the performance of the services themselves or even to distinguish the services from the traditions and precepts of the profession. Unlike most commercial products or even the services of other professions, which usually take tangible form, accounting services are invested with a degree of abstract trust and credibility that borders on the ethereal. Efforts to market them must take cognizance of this. Therefore, while I first considered setting forth the marketing concepts per se—no more, no less—I soon decided that they had to be presented in the context of the stuff and substance of the profession itself, including a history of auditing in a marketing perspective. I hope the reader persists through these sections, for while they are probably not as exciting as marketing, public relations, or communications, they are essential to an understanding of accountancy's marketplace.

It is a most unusual marketplace, by the way. It ultimately encompasses practically everyone. While lawyers are responsible to their clients and doctors to their patients, accountants seem to be responsible to just about everyone who relies on their reports.

The success of the profession's future marketing efforts will probably require a greater sensitivity to the changing needs of this marketplace than was exhibited in the past.

I believe this book will prove particularly informative to accounting students because of its marketing approach to describing the profession—how it appears to its publics as contrasted with how it views itself. For there has been a marked disparity between the profession's self-image and its public image. No doubt the next generation will see the two brought into closer harmony.

The book should also prove helpful to small and medium-sized firms in mounting a marketing effort. For it describes *how it is done,* while leaving ample room for the user to apply his own imagination and creativity. This is in gentle contrast with the more precise *how to do it* checklist approach, which I believe would not be quite as appropriate for thoughtful professionals.

Large firms may find the work useful in orienting staff members about the profession and in developing them into rounded, market-conscious professionals. In any event it purports to describe in some degree what these firms have been doing in marketing their services. I may have erred in some respects; for details about firm promotional practices are hard to come by, as my researcher found when he sought samples of firm promotional literature in the AICPA library. There were practically none—which may reflect past ethics prohibitions more than anything else. The large firms have always been generous in sharing their technical knowledge and expertise with others in the profession. Perhaps the newly relaxed ethics precepts will now permit them to share their promotional know-how as well.

I have relied a great deal on memory and personal notes-to-the-file for much of the background material and the events described, although John Carey's book, *The Rise of the Accounting Profession,* supplied several details I had forgotten. And *Professional Accounting in 25 Countries,* which I helped produce in 1964, provided information concerning particular United Kingdom Companies Acts that spawned the need for an independent profession. Both of these works were published by the American Institute of CPAs.

Also, some of the material included has appeared in the past in other form—in publications or manuals of my firm, Coopers & Lybrand, or in the booklet *Lybrand: A View from the Seventies* which I wrote to introduce new recruits to the profession. The firm has granted me permission to reuse these past writings.

Finally, I have omitted any discussion of advertising. While the former ethics prohibitions have been lifted, it is too early to conjecture the direction the advertising of professional accounting services will take. Conceivably it could be limited to simple "cards." But it is not difficult to envisage accounting firms resorting to more elaborate advertising, particularly if the stockholders of publicly-owned companies become more directly involved in the selection of auditors, as suggested in Chapter 12. But that seems pretty remote.

JAMES J. MAHON

May 1978

Contents

PART IV   A FIRMWIDE MARKETING FUNCTION

Tables and Exhibits

THE MARKETING OF PROFESSIONAL ACCOUNTING SERVICES

PART I

THE BASICS OF
SELLING PROFESSIONAL
SERVICES

CHAPTER 1

Professional Services Must Be Marketed, Too

Almost 15,000 young people, both men and women, enter public accounting each year. Some join established professional firms and serve existing clients. Others hang out a shingle and announce the availability of their services to the public.

Sooner or later these new professionals become concerned with building or expanding their professional practices, through either attracting new clients or through furnishing additional services to existing clients.

But only a handful know how to go about this sort of thing. Few professional schools offer courses on the marketing of professional services, or on the economics of practice. This is left largely to chance, with the result that the best equipped graduates from a technical viewpoint are often less than successful from a financial viewpoint—principally for lack of selling ability or effort.

Sometimes the philosophic background of one's profession is permitted to get in the way and unnecessarily inhibit efforts to expand the practice. This can be a serious psychological deterrent. All the professions, especially the learned ones, have long disavowed profits as a principal objective. Each has professed a loftier purpose or ideal—a philosophic obligation to apply its knowledge and experience toward improving mankind's condition in a spirit of genuine service. This ideal has been drilled into students in all the professions. The medical student has been infused with a zeal to protect health and alleviate pain. The law student has been inculcated with respect for the law and its importance in maintaining order. And integrity in reporting has been impressed upon the accountant as a foundation for economic decision-making. But until recently, financial rewards have seldom been mentioned—they were deemed a mere by-product of devotion to public service.

This traditional anti-commercialism has been reflected in the prohibitions against competitive bidding and advertising that have long been part of professional codes of ethics, although these are being relaxed of late. (See the Metcalf Committee's Recommendations in Chapter 9.) Blatant efforts to promote oneself economically or enlarge one's practice are considered unworthy of the dedicated professional. The predominant ethic has been that growth in a professional practice must be the product of reputation and the quality of service rendered.

This is changing. Financial rewards are becoming more important to members of the professions and to those aspiring to become members. Profits are now pursued in professional practice, and firms are organized and operated to produce profits. At the same time, the traditional philosophic precepts continue to be proclaimed, and they generally govern the standards of professional behavior and performance. In the minds of some, the new emphasis on financial emoluments conflicts with the traditional philosophic precepts. This, no doubt, has worked to inhibit marketing efforts.

Actually, there is no fundamental conflict between the desirability of maintaining a professional image on the one hand and the need to take appropriate steps to enlarge one's practice on the other. It is only necessary that the steps be appropriate, tasteful, and in harmony with the profession's traditional dignity and image. Indeed, far from hindering growth efforts, the professional aura, when delicately exploited, can be the single most important element in marketing professional services.

Public confidence and respect for a profession, its integrity, its independence, and its competence, are essential to growth. Professional canons of ethics or rules of conduct are generally designed to further this image. Careful adherence to the rules through years of exemplary service and conduct, and letting the public know this, are in themselves public relations acts of the highest order.

But some overt actions are also required if the practice is to grow. These invariably are selling or promotional in nature, even though the terms themselves may be considered repugnant in some professional quarters. Selling concepts are just as applicable to professional growth as they are to commercial development. Indeed, it is unlikely that any professional firm has ever become large without using some form of selling or promotion; and no large professional firm has ever remained large once it has stopped selling—in an appropriate way, of course.

A look at the history of any successful professional firm will confirm this. In addition to the necessary technical competence and the other basic requisites for professional growth, there usually will be found a "salesman" or several "salesmen" who are responsible for bringing in most of the new business. Ideally, the salesman is a knowledgeable member of his profession—a capable practitioner. But, consciously or otherwise, he adapts and applies the same techniques in obtaining visibility for himself and his firm and in selling professional services, as are used by the successful manufacturer or retailer.

Such a professional may not be aware that his activities are simply adaptations of traditional promotional or selling activities. He may not be able to either describe the techniques he uses or to explain his success. Frequently, he will attribute his new business record to personal qualities that he may or may not possess.

But whether he realizes it or not, he is nonetheless a salesman—one who uses positive selling techniques. His presence in a firm will invariably make the difference between a static practice and a dynamically expanding one.

Also, otherwise successful and prosperous professional

firms sometimes falter. They strike a plateau in growth—or they even retrogress. Curiously, this often occurs in the second generation, after the founder has retired or passed on. Founders of successful firms are often natural salesmen. But they are sometimes not aware of selling principles per se and cannot impart their knowledge to those who follow. And it is astonishing how often a first generation business-getter will select as his successor a technician who is skilled in servicing business that is developed by others, but who cannot sell. Thus the second generation of many firms is marked by technical richness—and promotional poverty. Until new selling talent appears, a hiatus in growth will invariably set in, while more aggressive competitors continue to forge ahead.

Whether they want to develop a professional practice from scratch or to accelerate the growth of an existing one, professionals should learn to market and sell their services— in an appropriate way. They should be able to attract and retain worthwhile clients.

Techniques for promoting and selling professional accounting services are described in this book. These techniques are applicable to any type of professional or personal service firm of any size, ranging from the sole practitioner to the world-wide firm. The principles are the same; modification may be required only in their application.

The need for internal communications may be met, in a national accounting firm, by using an elaborate house magazine replete with professionally designed graphics—or in a small firm, by having the senior partner write a simple memorandum. Or a large firm may keep its clients informed of important developments in the tax field through a printed client newsletter, while the sole practitioner may contact his clients through a personal letter or even a phone call. In all cases the basic aim of communicating useful information to clients or friends is a valid one. Only the modes need differ, and then only in degree.

Actually, communications skills are very important in developing a practice. Speaking or writing are most frequently used, but graphics or even "the silent language"—one's appearance, gestures or actions—can also be involved. An understanding of communications is vital to the accountant who is striving to build a practice.

These are discussed in Chapter 3.

But he also needs to be steeped in his profession and its services, particularly their applications and benefits—for they are the product.

And he should be familiar with the markets for accounting services and aware of their changing needs and attitudes.

Finally, he should know what is involved in a full-blown marketing and public relations function for a major firm.

But first—the basics of selling professional services.

CHAPTER 2

It Takes a Professional
To Sell Professional Services

Roger was in his middle thirties when he was admitted to partnership in his accounting firm. He had spent 10 years on the firm's audit staff and was in charge of several sizeable audit engagements. He was a student of accounting and was thoroughly familiar with the latest releases of the SEC, the Accounting Principles Board, and the various committees on auditing procedure of the American Institute of CPAs.

Roger lived in a prosperous suburban community, where he and his wife were active in church and civic affairs and their children attended public schools. He gained a little publicity when he was elected a trustee of his alma mater, an up–and–coming private college located only a few miles away. Otherwise, he had a low public profile. He was essentially modest, reserved, and somewhat formal. He was not given to flamboyancy or pushing himself into the center of things.

His greatest frustration, he confided one day to his senior partner, was that he had never obtained a new client for the firm. His partner, an experienced business-getter, replied, "You will, Roger. You are presentable, you are active in your community, and you are meeting potential clients every day. All you have to do is to quietly let them know *who* you are and *what* you do."

"One of these days," the older partner counseled, "one of these people will have an accounting or tax problem and will tell you about it. That will provide an opening for you to tell him *how* you and the firm can help him."

"In the meantime," the older man continued, "you should simply concentrate on enlarging your acquaintance-ship and making yourself known. "And Roger," he added, "if any of your friends don't know that you are a CPA and a partner in a prominent accounting firm—if they vaguely associate you with banking or brokerage or insurance or some other occupation—then you're simply not communicating; you're not getting across."

Roger proceeded to follow this advice within the limits of his quiet personality. He liked bowling and joined the Church's bowling league. The captain of his team, George, was the controller of a fair-sized pharmaceutical company whose stock was traded on the New York Stock Exchange.

The two became close friends. George had an accounting background too, so the conversation naturally turned to accounting at times. George asked Roger's views on the new accounting releases and other developments in the profession, an area in which Roger felt comfortable and confident. Although not loquacious generally, he warmed to these accounting questions. His replies reflected his enthusiasm for the subject and his desire to help George. They also revealed his basic integrity and dedication to principle.

During the bowling season, George developed a genuine respect for Roger as a professional accountant.

One evening after the season had ended and their team had won the league championship, George called Roger at home and said, "I wasn't free to tell you this before, Roger, but my company for some time has been planning to engage new auditors. I recommended you and your firm to our Board, and they would like to pursue this with you."

After a brief survey of the company's auditing requirements, Roger and several of his associates met with members of the Board; they outlined how they would approach the assignment and quoted an estimated fee. The firm was engaged as the company's new auditors.

Roger, with a newly acquired confidence in his ability to sell professional services, promptly went about attracting two more prospects, who became clients within the following 2 or 3 months.

Jerry was a lawyer and a CPA. He was a partner in an accounting firm, where he specialized in taxes. He was particularly well versed in the various types of real estate ventures that offered substantial tax advantages for individual investors.

He was also an avid golfer. He had an 8 handicap. In fact, this ability was to bring him into contact with one of golf's all time greats, who ultimately engaged him as his business and tax advisor. But that is another story.

One Saturday morning, Jerry picked up a game with a fellow club member, who happened to be the chairman and principal stockholder of a well-known manufacturer of paper products. Jerry told him *who* he was and *what* he did. The Chairman was a mediocre golfer, but this did not affect Jerry's game or his affability. He played well and responded willingly to his older companion's requests for advice concerning his golf swing.

As the two reached an area far removed from the clubhouse, a severe thunderstorm broke. They scrambled for a nearby shelter to sit out the storm. In these rustic surroundings, with the rain pounding overhead, the conversation turned to many things, including investments in real estate tax shelters. The Chairman, who was in a high tax bracket, was naturally interested. Jerry told him *how* he could help him. A meeting was arranged in which Jerry reviewed the Chairman's overall financial and tax picture and offered suggestions for improving it. These were well received, and in time Jerry's firm was engaged to be the company's auditors as well.

John began to specialize in taxes immediately after acquiring the requisite audit experience for a CPA certificate and passing the examination. He became completely immersed in tax work, and he wrote and spoke extensively on tax matters. He wrote several tax books that became standards in their field. He headed tax study committees and testified concerning proposed tax legislation. His reputation as a tax authority extended beyond his own profession. He also became known and respected within the legal profession, and frequently worked with top lawyers on the affairs of mutual clients.

One day while John was working with Monty, a partner in a large law firm, the conversation turned to personal matters, and they discovered a mutual interest in music. Both apparently had earned their way through school by playing in dance bands. John played saxophone, and Monty played trumpet. One Sunday Monty called John and asked him to substitute for the regular saxophonist in a small dance band that was rehearsing for a charity engagement at the local country club. John joined in the rehearsal. He filled in adequately in the absence of the regular sax man. Several recordings were made by the group, and the members enjoyed listening to the playbacks.

Several months after their artistically satisfying experience Monty was asked by one of his clients to recommend auditors. He suggested John's firm, and the firm was engaged after the customary meetings with management to determine the nature and scope of the engagement and to reach agreement on the fee.

These three cases were only slightly atypical. They contained most of the elements necessary for the successful sale of professional accounting services.

All of the accountants possessed the requisite professional qualifications and the technical expertise—one in auditing, and the others in taxes.

All had the necessary educational and cultural qualifications to merit acceptance in the marketplace where they sold their professional services—a suburban church, a golf club, and a prominent lawyer's office.

All made initial contact with the prospect by being present and active in the particular marketplace.

All discovered a mutual interest or shared an experience with the prospect which established a rapport and provided a basis for future communications—through bowling and winning the league championship, golfing and sitting out a storm in a rustic shelter, and playing music.

And all inspired the prospect with the requisite confidence that they and their firm could handle the professional assignment well.

But above all, the cases demonstrate that it takes a professional to sell professional services, whether he is an individual practitioner or a member of a firm. In a firm it is easier, of course. A firm can supply its members and associates with behind-the-scenes direction, ideas, and encouragement, as well as information and research concerning a prospect's company or its industry. It can help to create client demand and "open the door" with printed directories, newsletters, and technical publications. It can furnish the props and "bullets" to aid in making an effective new business presentation.

But ultimately it is the professional himself who must make contact with the prospect, hear out his problems, and convince him of his or his firm's capacity to solve them. His ability to sell derives more from his technical knowledge and experience than from his knowledge of selling and communications. But he cannot relegate the selling task to salesmen or other laymen—for the important element of client confidence would be missing. This is the type of confidence that a satisfied patient has in his doctor or that a client has in his lawyer. Such confidence can be communicated or inspired only by the professional himself.

The ability to communicate confidence varies from professional to professional. But it can be acquired or developed by gaining an understanding of the nature of communications and by learning how to communicate effectively. For confidence is a communication—and communicating is the key to developing a professional practice.

CHAPTER 3

Learning To Communicate Effectively

Unlike accounting and taxes, communications is not a discipline. It is neither structured nor orderly; rather, it is vague and amorphous. The term "communications" is in fact a Twentieth Century buzz word that has been applied to the telephone, the telegraph, the movies, and radio and television, as well as to newspapers, books, and magazines. It has been applied to data processing, printing, publishing, photography, and graphics, and to speaking and writing—as well as to music, painting, and the other fine arts. The term is sometimes used as a substitute for public relations, as, for example, in corporate communications and financial communications.

It is difficult to get at the root of this multifaceted phenomenon and to define its basic attributes—particularly those relevant to building a professional accounting practice.

True artists, of course, have never required a definition of communications in order to practice their art. Their abilities come naturally, and these have been applied liberally through the years to influence human history and culture. Churchill's talents for example, were essentially in communications, and he attributed his success in leading England through World War II to these abilities. He stated, "I have never accepted what many people have kindly said, namely, that I inspired the nation. Their will was resolute and remorseless and it proved unconquerable. It fell to me to express it and if I found the right word you must remember that I have always earned my living by the pen and by my tongue."

But to non-artists, non-communicators, businessmen, and indeed *accountants* who are interested in effective communications, definitions are important, if only to help zoom in on the subject and avoid scattering valuable messages to the four winds.

THE NATURE OF COMMUNICATIONS

Peter Drucker threw new light on the nature of communications in a paper entitled "Information, Communications and Understanding" which he delivered in Tokyo in 1969. Curiously, his definition of communications focused on what is received, rather than on what is uttered or transmitted.

Drucker describes a communication as a feeling, a sensation, or a perception *that is received*. It is conditioned more by the receiver's cultural background and emotions than by his intellect. It requires the receiver's involvement and is limited to what he expects or is conditioned to perceive—it must be within his range of perception or "wavelength."

Interestingly, Drucker classifies a "communication" as something beyond mere information, which he considers logical and impersonal. He notes that communications are not always deliberate or intentional, and that they are frequently multi-leveled. He points to works of art, for example, that can communicate on several levels, such as the literal, the metaphorical, the allegorical, or the symbolic—all of which can evoke differing emotions in different viewers.

Pursuing the Drucker idea, it is apparent that the transmission which "communicates" is *itself* an emotion that evokes the spark of response in the recipient. Thus a friendly smile, a warm handclasp, a loving touch, or a pleasant remark "communicates." One's appearance, gestures, or actions, that is, the silent language, also communicates. So does music and art. A notable experience shared with another can be a powerful communication. However, bare words, whether spoken or written, do not communicate—within the Drucker concept. They *do* convey information or knowledge. But to truly communicate, words must be laced with some sort of emotion—energy, inspiration, sincerity, compassion, enthusiasm, excitement, ardor, sorrow, anger, indignation. These transform the words from the status of mere information to one of "communication."

Apparently, the capacity to "utter" an emotion which will communicate is possessed by virtually everyone, with varying degrees of talent and sophistication, ranging from the hungry baby's cry for food or the impassioned orator's appeal for action, to the inspired artist's symbolical message. Genuine poetry, it is said, can communicate before it is understood.

Now, by excluding "mere information" from his concept of communications, Drucker ignores much of the technical material with which accountants deal in their professional reports and statements. This does not mean that the information in an accountant's report is not understood by the reader. The information most assuredly *is* received and understood by the interested reader—and it has value. Even a bare stock market quotation or earnings-per-share projection can be received and understood. And a mere directory will convey information.

Rather, Drucker's exclusion of information from the communications category reflects an attempt to carve out a small part of the communications universe—the emotion-laden part—in order to better deal with it. That he elected to apply the broad term "communication" to this fractional concept is curious.

Nevertheless, an understanding of that concept is valuable in developing a professional practice because it helps to explain the element of *confidence* which lies at the root of the professional relationship.

Confidence–The Professional's Ultimate Communication

Confidence is a perfect example of a meaningful communication. It is a client's belief—or feeling, sensation, or perception—that the professional can take a problem off the client's shoulders and onto his own. Confidence begins to build in a prospective client when the professional manifests an understanding of his problem and communicates his capacity to solve it. This process may be initiated in various types of audiences or forums, with appropriate messages or utterances conveyed through suitable media or modes—as, for example, through a speech on income taxes by an accountant at a Rotary Club luncheon. The initial confidence ultimately ripens into a viable professional relationship, with the all important personal contact between the professional and the client that is the essence of such relationships.

Thus given the requisite professional competence and technical knowledge, the professional builds his practice by attracting prospective clients through appropriate visibility techniques, by acquiring an understanding of their particular needs or problems, and by personally convincing them of his ability to solve them. But the effectiveness of all of these ultimately depends on the individual professional's ability to inspire or to communicate confidence. What follows is designed to help the professional accountant communicate effectively. This is the key to selling professional services, whether one is an individual practitioner or part of a large firm.

Audiences and forums appropriate for gaining professional visibility are described herinafter and the media and modes suitable for reaching these audiences are evaluated. Speaking and writing are singled out for special comment because of their vital importance in developing and maintaining a professional accounting practice. Also singled out for comment are the requisites for gaining acceptance in society's leadership echelons, the ultimate marketplace.

Finally, suggestions for making an effective proposal and presentation and "clinching" the new client are presented.

IMPORTANCE OF SPEAKING AND WRITING ABILITIES

Ordinarily, technical knowledge alone is not enough to assure success in a profession; an ability to communicate that knowledge to others is needed. This requires proficiency in speaking and writing—especially the former. Indeed, the ability to speak well is probably the single most important factor needed to achieve success in a profession. The heights attained by top labor leaders of the past are ample evidence of the sheer value of public speaking, since most had little formal education or training. The same speaking ability in highly educated professionals can speed their progress remarkably—particularly if they are staff accountants aspiring for partnership in their firm.

Ordinary speaking and writing abilities are intrinsic to professional practice, and one must have some knowledge of both before being admitted to any of the recognized professions. Nevertheless, there is a wide disparity among professionals in even ordinary speaking and writing abilities because of their differing cultural and educational backgrounds and varying degrees of natural talent.

And while it is difficult to define the minimum technical knowledge that should be possessed by a professional accountant, he certainly should be able to impart this knowledge and information accurately and with sufficient clarity to meet the day-to-day requisites of his practice. And he should be able to meet the speaking and writing cultural norms of the people he deals with in the daily pursuit of his professional work—particularly officers and directors of clients. Faulty diction or grammar, as Shaw pointed out in Pygmalion, can be a dead giveaway.

But it is the higher levels of speaking and writing— *public* speaking and writing for publication—that offer the greatest rewards for the professional. And, given average basic speaking and writing abilities, the ambitious accountant should endeavor to become proficient at these more sophisticated levels.

Public Speaking

A well organized and well delivered speech by a professional on a vital and timely subject can be an effective development tool.

Many accountants are effective speakers and writers

and are sought after by many organizations. This is partially because some firms encourage better speaking and writing and frequent public appearances—and reward those who do it well. They make formal speaking courses available to their people throughout the U. S. Hundreds of staff accountants take these courses; many become partners. And professional personnel are sometimes trained to participate effectively in client conferences and presentations by using films that simulate actual situations.

Of course, there ought not be any illusions about the value of public speaking courses. They cannot work miracles. They cannot turn everyone into a great speaker. But they can rid a person of audience fear and teach him how to give an acceptable talk or conduct a conference. They can assist him in speech construction, so that audience interest can be aroused and held for a reasonable length of time. A speaking course can train a person to be himself before an audience. It teaches him "expanded conversation," so to speak. At the completion of the course and with moderate practice, an individual can expect to appear before an audience as he is—that is, within the confines of his own personality.

One need not become an orator. One simply needs to develop the ability to communicate one's technical knowledge and expertise to others in an orderly manner—*and be believable.*

Believability is important. It is a product of the listener's expectations. Most audiences have a preconceived impression of accountants as being dull and unimaginative. Accountants are not expected to be great speakers or orators, and, if perchance they are, this actually could reduce their believability—since audiences become more carried away with their histrionic abilities than with their professional prowess. This is not to say that a professional with unusual speaking abilities should hide his talents. Rather, he should simply shape the pace and dignity of his talks to fit the expectations of the particular audiences. He should not over–perform.

Subjects treated by the accountant in his talks and other public utterances should not stray too far from the public's expectations. Such topics would include taxes, economics, management—and, of course, financial reporting. But they should not include anything as far removed as, say, the Salk vaccine. An accountant is not ordinarily expected to be authorative on such subjects, and any attempt to hold forth on them is bound to impugn his believability.

The Extempore Speech. From a professional accountant's viewpoint there are two principal types of speeches— the extempore speech and the written speech that is read to the audience. In junior high school there was also the memorized speech, but this is too risky for anyone but a professional actor who can remember lines or who has a prompter in the wings. And there is the impromptu speech that is an instant response to a toast or similar occasion. It is expressed in the words of the moment and is not ordinarily planned or thought out in advance.

The extempore speech is the most effective type. Most public speaking courses emphasize it. It is a previously planned presentation delivered in the words of the moment. Ordinarily the speaker follows an outline that he has noted on a card or has committed to memory. But the words, sentences, and paragraphs are developed on the spot—they are part of an ongoing cognitive process.

Extempore speaking "communicates" more effectively than any other form of speech, primarily because it is laced with the speaker's emotions and feelings of the moment, which he expresses through natural inflection and other voice nuances.

The extempore speech requires more thought and preparation than other types of talks. A broad outline must be evolved; for example, "the problem," "the solution," and "the call to arms." The detailed points must be filled in. And the whole presentation must be thought about and mulled over extensively up to the very time of its delivery. The more the speaker thinks about the topic he plans to discuss, the fresher his presentation and the greater its impact.

Mark Twain, when asked by an ardent admirer how he became such an effective speaker, reportedly replied, "I simply fill myself with my subject as one would fill a keg. And when I pull the bung it gushes out." The fact that an extempore speech is delivered in the words of the moment does not preclude the use of carefully arranged catch phrases or quotations. Winston Churchill was known to evolve some of his most frequently quoted phrases beforehand, noting them on the back of an envelope. One example: "Blood, sweat, and tears."

One problem with extempore speaking, of course, is the danger of talking overlong. A speaker should plan to stay within the time limits imposed on him by the program chairman, and, if there are none, he should adopt a time limit for himself and abide by it. If not disciplined, extempore talks can stretch on seemingly forever, with the speaker being the last to realize how tiresome he has become. The best extempore talks are those that compress two hours of subject matter into twenty minutes. This requires extensive preparation, but from the viewpoint of winning audience approval, it is well worth it.

The Written Speech. The written speech is the hardest to write and deliver effectively. It can be deadly in the hands of the amateur. And yet it is used extensively at business dinners and on other occasions by corporate executives who "do not wish to be misquoted," and by professional people who all too often take literally the invitation to "deliver a paper" at a technical or professional meeting. The almost invariable result is boredom.

There is a world of difference between writing for the ear and writing for print. The former is a highly specialized form of the writer's art. Indeed, even good print writers are not necessarily good speech writers. Unfortunately, most written speeches are written by print writers or by the speakers themselves. And they are invariably amateurish at best.

Also, there is a world of difference in impact between reading previously written words and sentences, no matter how well written, and expressing one's thoughts and ideas in the words of the moment. An amateur can get away with the latter, but it takes virtually a professional actor or narrator to read a speech effectively. The key, of course, is to comprehend the subject matter and to read thoughts rather than words. This promotes the natural inflection, emphasis, and cadence that is essential in oral communication. Indeed, even a professional narrator will put something of himself into a speech by altering or modifying the text to fit his style of expression. Walter Cronkite is said to rarely deliver from a script prepared by others without refashioning it for his own delivery.

Unless an accountant is unusually skilled in delivering from a text, he should avoid the written speech. If he has to supply a paper for publication, let him do it. But he should deliver the speech extempore from an outline prepared from the paper. For the two modes are vastly different.

Of course, one's reading delivery can be improved by practicing with a tape recorder. At first the playbacks will be dull and colorless. But as one learns to read thoughts rather than words and adds inflection at appropriate points, the rendition will become more expressive. Curiously, the more exaggerated the delivery into the electronic recorder, the more natural the output will sound.

However, unless the professional accountant wishes to devote the time necessary to developing professional-level communicating skills, he will be better off with the extempore type of speech. It makes him more believable.

Public Address Systems. Many public speaking teachers urge their students to ignore the public address system microphone they may find at the podium and to simply speak as though it were not there. The author's advice based on an extensive speaking career is exactly the opposite: don't ignore it—use it!

A good public address system can enlarge the impact

and enhance the effectiveness of a presentation significantly. It enables a speaker to reach the whole audience in his natural voice without undue effort.

There is a particular level of volume and pitch at which a voice is at its richest, phonetically—when all the overtones and harmonics in the vocal chords are in agreeable balance, and resonance is at its best. Ordinarily, this is at neither a shouting nor a whispering level, or at neither the highest nor the lowest pitch. It is somewhere between. It is the stage at which the voice is the most rounded, most flexible, most amenable to modulation, and most arresting. This stage can be determined for oneself by simply listening to one's voice in the earpiece of an ordinary telephone while speaking at various levels into the mouthpiece. Once the normal level is determined, the dramatic effect of changes in volume, pitch, and inflection can be heightened by moving the mouthpiece closer to and away from the mouth. A whisper can be made a spine–tingling roar.

The public address system should be approached as an enlarged telephone. Using "normal" speaking volume and pitch, the speaker should bring his mouth close enough to the microphone to be able to hear his voice through the public address speakers located throughout the room, and then should constantly modulate it to achieve the desired effect thereafter. He should not, however, "crowd" the microphone to the point of deafening volume or feedback noise. Once "tuned-in," he will find that the amplification will not only nudge him to articulate more clearly, but it will heighten the dramatic effect of inflection and changes in pitch, volume, and cadence. An amplified voice should not be a different voice—simply a larger one.

Articles and Papers

From a professional development viewpoint, it is hard to appraise the relative value of speeches versus articles and papers. A good speech probably has greater immediate impact. It creates a more vivid impression because of the added effect of the speaker's personality—and because more people seem to prefer listening to reading. On the other hand, a speaking audience is necessarily limited in size and duration (except, of course, for radio, television, and motion pictures, which are outside the scope of this work), whereas the reading audience has practically unlimited potential. It must be concluded that good speeches and good articles and papers have equal development value.

Much of what has been said about public speaking and speeches also applies to the development of writing abilities and the writing of publishable articles and papers by members of a profession. Membership in any profession involves an obligation to contribute to the improvement of the standards, skills, and knowledge of that profession. Sharing technical information with other members of the profession, or indeed, using it to enlighten or educate the general public is one way of meeting this obligation.

The collateral but important benefit that accrues to members of a profession from contributions to its literature is the enhancement of their professional stature and the recognition of their technical prowess outside the profession's ranks—that is, in the eyes of their clients, the members of other professions (e.g., lawyers), and the general public. Enhanced professional stature and recognition of technical prowess generate increased demand for services, with greater financial rewards.

Thus thoughtful papers and articles on timely, interesting, and provocative subjects upon which a professional accountant is particularly qualified to speak are an accepted major instrument of professional development. They establish and publicize the author in his particular field of endeavor, create a demand for his personal services, and reflect favorably on the firm with which he is associated.

Writing articles and papers on technical accounting subjects will not only increase an accountant's proficiency in an art that is essential to public accounting practice; it will also, when highly developed, be a potent instrument in his professional development.

Printed and other types of communications are described in Chapter 15, The Communications Function—Types of Communications and Messages.

CHAPTER 4

Forums for Gaining Visibility and Attracting New Clients

Activities and forums appropriate for gaining visibility vary among the professions, but there is some overlap. Meetings of business executives, for example, are a logical audience for both lawyers and consultants, as well as accountants. All three can be found on programs of business seminars.

Also, there is a rough relationship between the rank or standing of a professional and the prestige of the audience he can reasonably aspire to address. A junior accountant, for example, is not likely to be invited to make a major address before the prestigious Economic Club of New York, whereas the managing partner of a major firm may be. Ironically, the junior may be a much better speaker—but most program committees somehow consider this secondary! They invariably seek the head man with the important title, whether the poor fellow can speak or not. Also, in a large company the president's door may be wide open to the senior partner in an accounting firm, while the office of the controller is about as high as the junior partner can aspire to at that stage in his career. However, controllers *do* become presidents; they should not be taken too lightly!

Ordinarily the professional's opportunities for gaining visibility begin in the local chapter of his professional association or society. Young accountants, for example, can test their wings by moving up the chairs of the local chapter of the CPA society or the National Association of Accountants, progressing from there to positions in the corresponding state and national organizations. Recognition of a young accountant's professional prowess by his peers through election or appointment to office in the association, speeches made at its meetings, or articles published in its journals can spill over to lay audiences and enhance his reputation among those who would directly use his services. Indeed, some successful physicians, particularly those whose practice is built around referral patients, rely almost exclusively on the contacts made and visibility gained within. Dr. Denton Cooley, the famous heart surgeon, is an example. He regularly appears in medical seminars and symposiums throughout the world—and many of his patients are referred by physicians on whom he makes an impression at those meetings. But even doctors who are involved in primary patient care sometimes enhance their standing by the selective distribution of reprints of articles they have written for professional journals. Of course, the layman may not understand a highly technical medical article—but he may be impressed with the fact of its publication!

There is a pecking order among professional journals, too. A national journal, such as the *Journal of Accountancy,* is more apt to include articles written by the more prestigious members of the profession than, say, the *Spokesman,* the relatively modest journal of the Pennyslvania Institute of CPAs.

The American Bar Association's journal is also considered more prestigious than the state or local legal periodicals. Curiously, though, the regional *New England Journal of Medicine* is regarded as tops in its field—its prestige is said to be as great as that of any national journal. The *Harvard Business Review* enjoys similar standing in its field. In these cases editorial competence and publishing savvy no doubt have influenced the respective journals' ratings and prestige, although usually the size and extent of its geographic coverage governs a publication's relative standing.

THE SOCIAL CONTRIBUTION— THE DOOR TO PROFESSIONAL GROWTH

The activities and forums in which a professional accountant might participate in order to become favorably known in his community include alumni, church, club, and civic activities, as well as memberships in service clubs and in business and trade organizations. Many fruitful business and professional relationships have originated from friendships formed in this type of environment.

The greatest opportunities for growth in a profession depend on the extent to which the members contribute to society as a whole. Indeed, it is the presence of social consciousness in the profession, and the public's recognition of this, that forms the dividing line between a profession and a mere occupation.

Accountancy, for example, has long been referred to as a profession, although it has not been generally considered to be a learned profession on the same plane as the medical or legal professions.

This disparity was studied in 1956 for the American Institute of CPAs by Arthur Tourtellot of Earl Newsome and Company. He found that, although accountancy possessed all the internal characteristics of a profession such as a body of specialized knowledge and recognized educational standards, it lacked the requisite *external* characteristics—the acceptance of the social responsibility inherent in an occupation endowed with a public interest, and the existence of an organization devoted to the advancement of the social obligation, as distinct from the economic interest of the group.

The Tourtellot report emphasized that it is these latter characteristics that are most influential in the public's judgments of professions. And he urged the accounting profession to undertake public service projects in areas where its experience and knowledge would lend economic order and stability. Implicit in his recommendation was that professional accounting should not only perform good works, but it should get credit for them. This, of course, is one definition of public relations—"to do good and get credit for it."

Actually, the accounting profession has been performing good works in the public interest for many years. Accountants have served on governmental expenditure task forces and tax reform study groups, and have testified regularly at Legislative Committee hearings in connection with proposed legislation. They have participated in trade missions and other activities to stimulate business activity. They have participated in programs to improve financial reporting abroad and to help developing countries realize the benefits of orderly accounting. And accounting firms have intermittently sponsored studies of matters vital to the public interest. A firm–sponsored study of the late 1960s, "Towards A Certificateless Society," sought to find a solution for the mounting paper work problem of investors and the securities industry. A 1976 study, "Financial Disclosure Practices of American Cities," was designed to help cities reestablish their financial credibility. And a hypothetical balance sheet of the Federal government demonstrated the magnitude of the government's unfunded commitments.

In the final analysis, it is probably the profession's contributions in these types of public interest situations that produce the greatest growth. And these of course should be done gratuitously and for their own sake, even though they may lead to tangible monetary reward.

The contributions need not have national implications. They may relate to state or even local socio-economic problems in which the analytical abilities and technical skills of the professional accountant can contribute to a solution.

At the very least, an accountant should seek positions of leadership in such civic organizations as the Chamber of Commerce, the Community Chest, the Boy Scout movement, or the Y.M.C.A., where he will rub elbows with top management in dealing with local, civic, public, and business problems.

And he should not shun the opportunities for publicity that naturally are associated with these works or affiliations. While the canons of professional ethics may frown upon the seeking of publicity for its own sake, they have never discouraged hard news stories that reflect favorably upon the profession or its members. If the accountant's contribution to the public interest is broad enough and generous enough, it will be acclaimed by a grateful public. And an old adage will surely obtain . . . "one gets paid the most for that which he does for nothing."

Government Legislative and Administrative Committee Hearings

Testimony before legislative and administrative committees on subjects within their spheres of technical knowledge affords professional accountants an opportunity to contribute to the public interest. This is true especially of proposed legislation or regulations on federal, state, and local taxes; on accounting requirements and procedures; and on business operations. Accountants often testify before governmental hearing committees as representatives of professional accounting societies (e.g., AICPA), civic and business organizations (e.g., Chambers of Commerce), industry or trade organizations (e.g., American Mining Congress), or on their own behalf as "friends of the court."

In addition to their socio-economic benefits, these appearances promote prestige in the eyes of clients and the general business community.

In such appearances a prepared statement is usually read at the hearing, with copies available for the printed record and representatives of the press. Testimony is ordinarily not extempore, except for replies to questions raised at the hearing. Naturally, any statements should be as objective and as circumspect as possible.

Stockholders' Meetings

A stockholders' meeting of a client company, particularly a publicly held company, is a potentially valuable forum for an accountant and his firm, because most of these meetings are attended by people whose good will can be valuable. These include top management, large stockholders (who often are also large stockholders in other companies as well), bankers, investment bankers, brokers, underwriters, and managers of large mutual funds. Moreover, public attention has been increasingly focused on stockholders' meetings by the financial press because of the increasing prevalance of proxy fights and the presence of vociferous professional minority stockholders.

The independent auditors are ordinarily the least vocal of those present at stockholders' meetings—probably because traditionally their participation has been limited to answering questions directed to them by professional minority stockholders. Yet, they have an intimate knowledge of the company's financial affairs and are in a position to help reduce disputes resulting from misunderstanding or distortion of facts.

The stockholders' meeting is a distinct opportunity for an accountant to help cement company–shareholder relations—and incidentally to place himself and his firm in the best possible light with both management and stockholders. Moreover, the day is coming when independent accountants will be selected more directly by stockholders or stockholders' committees—instead of by management, or even directors. Accountants should prepare for this by laying the groundwork for broad stockholder appeal, making evident their knowledge of the company's affairs as well as their expertise on sound accounting practices.

Whenever an occasion arises for an accountant to give a verbal presentation, it should be appropriately exploited. "Questions to the auditors" should be anticipated, and answers carefully prepared and discussed beforehand with management. Simple "yes" or "no" answers should be avoided. Rather, the accountant should welcome an opportunity to air a subject concisely but frankly, to throw light on it, and to educate concerning it—not for the sole benefit of the professional minority stockholder, but for the benefit of everyone present, particularly the other stockholders. His remarks should be fair, objective, and consistent with his role as an independent auditor. His presentation should be pleasing, but not defensive. And he should not give the appearance of taking sides either for or against management.

MOVING INTO THE LEADERSHIP ECHELONS

While technical knowledge is basic to the sale of professional services, a grasp of the broad social environment is not only expected, but essential for a top accountant. And while a young accountant's early career may concentrate on acquiring technical knowledge and skills and developing maturity and judgment, his later years will call for greater emphasis on the cultural and social aspects of his expanding environment. Knowledge gained in his undergraduate studies in science, the arts, and the humanities then assume new meaning. His courses in ethics, philosophy, sociology, psychology, literature, and history acquire more importance. So do the so-called social graces that were drummed into him by his parents and later polished through associations in his academic and early working years.

What the accountant needs, of course, is the confidence to move gracefully at any of the various levels of modern society—all of which are represented in accounting clienteles. Client executives range from self-educated, rugged individualists to highly cultured blue bloods, and they embrace all nationalities, colors, and creeds. The accountant will want to learn to meet all of these people on their own grounds—and to be comfortable with them, and they with him.

And as he goes up the professional ladder, his "publics" will expand beyond client personnel to others in the community who may or may not have a direct relationship with his firm or its clientele—bankers, lawyers, educators, government officials, and even executives of non-clients. The proportion of his contacts and associations in these non-client areas can normally be expected to increase as his position in the community expands.

His wife's role in cultivating these associations will assume more importance as he moves from an exclusively business-oriented environment to a more rounded recreational, cultural, and social environment. Actually, if his sole purpose were the development of potential business relationships, he could do as well in the cultural and social community as in the business community. Human relations, of course, are the particular forte of women—whether they are bringing up a family or pursuing a professional or business career of their own. Given encouragement, a wife will usually perceive the centers of cultural and social activity and will move her husband and her family toward professionally meaningful relationships.

If experience in developing such relationships has any meaning, however, it suggests the desirability of proceeding at a modest pace, particularly in dealing with the so-called higher echelons. Over-aggressiveness or "pushiness" is frequently resented. Family background and old school ties are still important to some, even in America, although acceptance can usually be traced to significant accomplishments in government, business, the professions, or the arts. Society is, after all, pluralistic as well as upwardly mobile. And acceptance is not based entirely on family background or economic affluence. Contributions to the social order count very heavily.

The key lies in accomplishment—accomplishment in any respected field of endeavor. Ordinarily, accomplishment is first recognized and acknowledged by peers in one's particular field. Attainment of partnership in an important accounting firm is a significant accomplishment. So is becoming president of a professional society, or chairman of a major committee. And, of course, the authorship of recognized works in one's field is a mark of leadership.

Leaders in all fields are invariably drawn together in some form of social or recreational fraternization; in a city or country club, for example. They cooperate in broad environmental and civic activities as well, and ultimately constitute the leadership in the community, the state, or even the nation. They are the true "establishment." While there are sometimes snobbish overtones in this fraternization, basic accomplishment is more important, although the sledding would be tougher if one were unaware of, or ignored, accepted standards of personal grooming or behavior. This is not to say that the rare genius cannot get away with some eccentricities of behavior. But, lacking genius, one would be well advised to play by the rules of the game.

Abilities or accomplishments outside of one's principal field of endeavor are equally important in achieving leadership. Leadership implies breadth of knowledge and versatility of talents. Knowledge of the interrelationships among the many elements in the vast socio-economic culture and the ability to analyze, evaluate, and articulate the possible future impact of new developments is important. Indeed, broad knowledgeability is itself a major accomplishment. Da Vinci, Marx, Rivera, Keynes, Gershwin, and even the Beatles, effected significant social changes in the past. And the works of John XXIII, McLuhan, Drucker, and Gardner no doubt portend future change. Although essentially a financial and business newspaper, the *Wall Street Journal* has been expanding its social-cultural content for years. And the *New York Times* has always been multi-dimensional.

At leadership levels a person must be knowledgeable in more than one dimension. Churchill was a writer and an artist as well as a statesman; Eisenhower wrote a major work in history—"Crusade in Europe;" and David Rockefeller is a renowned collector and benefactor of fine arts. Such talents and interests mark the broader person, the rounder personality—the leader.

These talents and interests also serve as "levers of acceptance." Many major clients emerge from contacts developed during the pursuit of a hobby or other activity—bowling, golf, tennis, sailing, hunting, painting, and music.

Actually, an accountant should sharpen up *all* his abilities and talents and put them to use. They will reflect all the dimensions of the rounded professional.

A large accounting practice is developed primarily

through the efforts of multi-dimensional people—people who work at developing all their abilities. Someone once called it "culture"—an imperative to high professional attainment. It goes without saying that such attainment implies economic rewards. Society puts a high premium on quality.

CHAPTER 5

Retaining Present Clients and Clinching New Ones

Attracting and clinching a substantial new client can be infinitely satisfying, but not, however, at the expense of losing a substantial existing client. For then *two* new clients would be needed to grow—one to replace the old client and the other to achieve growth. Yet successful new business producers in the accounting profession sometimes become so enamored with the thrill of the chase for new clients that they neglect the old ones.

Existing clients are the single most important factor in professional growth. As "satisfied customers," they constitute a formidable group that can further the accountant's interests by recommending him to other clients. Indeed, as stated elsewhere in this work, over 50% of the new clients obtained by some firms result from referrals by existing clients.

The aim, therefore, should be to develop among existing clients, a single frame of mind—as inspired, near–dedicated boosters of their accountants, intensely proud to be among their clients, and unabashedly vocal in extolling their virtues to friends and colleagues who may be associated with other companies or enterprises.

To maintain this almost religious fervor, clients must be continuously "sold." It is not enough to sell them only once—when they were acquired. The selling effort must persist during the entire association with the client. The accountant and everyone in his organization must convey the "welcome message" to every client at every opportunity—to let him know that he is highly regarded by his accounting firm.

How is this done? Mostly by actions and attitudes—as constrasted with mere words.

SERVING EXISTING CLIENTS

The key to holding clients, of course, is service that is valuable and efficient. What constitutes a "valuable" service will vary from client to client. What may be valuable to a small company may have little application to a large one. And the principal concerns of the president of a large company may be quite different from those of an outside member of his board. These will be examined later.

Client Expectations

All clients however, expect a professional accountant to look and behave like a professional. This is a matter of dress, grooming, culture, manners, disposition, diction, and other personal attributes and behavior. Norms and customs differ, of course, between companies, industries and locations. Dress, for example, varies widely. While accountants at one time were required to dress formally for all client contacts, today they seek merely to conform with the highest standard prevailing in the particular client's place of business.

As pointed out in Chapter 11, The Industry Markets, clients expect an accountant to be familiar with their types of businesses and their jargon from his first appearance on the premises. One electric utility controller has complained that he has to spend too much time "educating" new staff accountants on the rudiments of his company, when a brief industry orientation session by their firm might have prepared them beforehand.

Clients also expect the accountant to go quietly and efficiently about his business, with as little disruption as possible to their organization; to specify early what books, records, or other data he will require during the engagement;

and to perform the work in minimum time by time budgeting and other efficiencies. And they expect him to be close-mouthed about their business and not to discuss it with their employees or others—except of course for the information that is conveyed in audited financial statements.

Clients expect the accountant's work to be complete, thorough and "well-packaged,"

The art of report writing and presentation, of course, is a subject in itself. It is sufficient to say here that a report should sell itself; it should be pleasing to the eye; it should seduce the reader and hold him to the end. Actually, the graphics potential of even typewritten reports has scarcely been tapped. This subject is well worth the attention of professionals—whose reports often look and read like dust-covered dissertations from the 1890s.

Clients expect their accountants to be sensitive to their particular needs and to concentrate on these. There is no reason to perform superflous services or to supply useless information. But constructive suggestions or financial comments that ensue from the work itself should be passed on gratuitously to the client—particularly ideas that will improve the client's profits. Every annual audit report, for example, should be followed by a separate letter or report containing comments on financial and operating ratios or similar matters, in addition to the customary letter commenting on internal controls. And while it may seem self-serving, accountants should be alert to opportunities to perform special studies or analyses for the client—cost reduction studies, tax minimization plans or product line profitability studies—engagements that will produce immediate client benefits measurable in dollars.

Clients expect their accountants to keep them informed of developments in business or government that would affect them—changes in the tax law; new laws or regulations that impose new compliance requirements (for example, ERISA); new management methods and techniques; and new markets and other opportunities. Notifying the client personally about these developments and noting how they will affect him is the most effective way of conveying this information. But, of course, as clienteles become larger and more varied, this becomes more difficult, and letters or even printed newsletters must be resorted to. When a development is significant and far reaching—when, for example, a major new tax act is passed—a client seminar might be set up at a local hotel, where firm experts can explain the new provisions to client personnel. (See Chapter 15, The Communications Function—Types of Communications and Messages.)

Finally, as normal human beings, clients will naturally respond to an accountant's exhibition of warm, sincere, and sympathetic personal interest in them and their problems. An accountant should plan to visit his client at least twice a year for this purpose alone. His professional experience and knowledge in all phases of business operation is usually extensive. he should give clients the full benefit of it and counsel them freely.

The special interests and concerns of specific client groups, such as individual income tax clients and proprietorships—as well as professional management, directors, and stockholders—are described in Chapter 12, The Publics.

RESPONDING TO A NEW CLIENT INQUIRY

The accountant's efforts to gain visibility in the marketplace should eventually result in some overture from a prospective client—a letter, a phone call, or a personal inquiry at a social or business function. Fielding that inquiry effectively and converting the prospect into a client is a point where many professionals fail, due to a lack of the confidence or selling ability needed to clinch a new engagement.

Unlike the three slightly atypical success stories described in Chapter 2, where the new clients were obtained with little selling effort by the accountant, the typical overture from a prospective client requires a strong, positive response from the accountant. If he exhibits a sincere interest in the prospect and his problem at that stage, he is well on his way to gaining a new client.

He should find out as much as possible in this initial contact who the prospect is, what his business is, what his problems are, and what type of service he will probably need. And he should promptly arrange a date as soon as possible to discuss the matter.

The accountant should prepare well for the preliminary meeting with the prospect and arm himself with as much advance information he can obtain about the prospect from Standard & Poors, Dun & Bradstreet reports, or other sources. He should decide who is going to attend the meeting and who will be the principal spokesman. While he will not wish to overwhelm the prospect, he should arrange for at least two representatives of the accounting firm to attend the meeting—including a specialist in the area of the prospect's expressed area of interest. Since he is apt to be working closely with the prospect, he should begin to earn the requisite client confidence at this stage.

The meeting may prove to be an informal oral proposal that will immediately result in a new engagement, with the terms of the arrangement and the amount of the estimated fee to be confirmed by letter. This is often the case when the prospect is a small or medium-size organization or when it is one with whom the accountant already has close personal connections.

When the prospect is a large company or institution, however, and particularly when it has invited proposals from other accounting firms, the preliminary meeting will invariably be followed by a survey of the prospect's needs, a formal written proposal, and a full dress oral presentation before a committee of management or the board of directors.

These are discussed in greater detail in Chapter 17, The New Client Proposal and Presentation. For the clinching of a substantial new client by a professional accounting firm is a major event. It is a spectacular result of extensive training, support efforts, and applied communications abilities. And it presupposes a knowledge of the product and its markets, as well as an understanding of the marketing concept as applied to professional firms.

PART II

THE PRODUCT-
—A DISTINGUISHED
PROFESSION
AND ITS SERVICES

CHAPTER 6

It's More Than Just Numbers

A requisite of successful salesmanship is knowing one's product, its applications, and its markets—and being able to articulate these.

Accountancy's product is intangible and complex. It is a professional service, but, unlike most professional services, which acquire an identity and utility of their own—a suture, a splint, a denture, a contract, or a will—accountancy's principal product, the attestation of financial reports, is but a blessing or benediction, the value of which depends entirely on the perceived character and reputation of the professional. The accountant's technical skills are important—but his credibility is everything.

To understand accountancy's product and its markets is to understand the accountant as a moral and objective creature and his profession as a philosophic force. The chapters following endeavor to portray the accountant, his profession, and accountancy's precepts in historical perspective—for accountancy's future is irretrievably intertwined with its past.

First, something about the nature of the work itself—working with numbers.

AGILITY WITH NUMBERS BASIC

While there is much more to accounting than numbers, they are basic to the art. Working with them at even the most rudimentary level can be fascinating. A sense of achievement can be derived merely from adding, subtracting, multiplying, and dividing numbers accurately. As everyone who has re-

conciled a bank statement knows, there is a feeling of satisfaction in "striking a balance." It is a little victory, a triumph
of order over disorder, something that calls for a small
celebration—like lighting a cigarette (before the Surgeon
General's warning!). As one accounting student put it, "I love
the way the trial balance always balances."

Pure numbers inspire respect. Unlike people, they behave perfectly. They respond to any proper command. And
they have a certain integrity which, when violated, seeks its
own redress. Which no doubt explains why a bookkeeper will
spend hours digging for a small error in the numbers rather
than compromising their integrity—or his own—by "plug-
ging the balance." The novice learns early, usually during the
first few weeks on the job, that, "if one puts figures down
right, and adds them up right, they'll come out right." He
finds that the more care he uses, the more satisfaction he
derives from his work. While accounting offers many rewards, there is a basic satisfaction in the work itself.

Naturally, the more one works with numbers, the
greater one's agility. Indeed, arithmetical prowess is considered basic to the experienced accountant, primarily because
it is his most visible ability. Despite the prevalence of the
portable adding machine and the pocket computer, adeptness with figures is still expected of the accountant. How
often he is asked by his friends to keep the golf score or
bridge score, or to add the restaurant bill or figure the proper shares of a split check. In fact, the accountant's highly
developed facility with figures invariably leads him to "audit"
every bill or statement presented to him—even if it's an adding machine tape!

Several years ago the cashier of a prominent Mexico
City hotel evolved a method of "painlessly" extracting an
extra 100 pesos, then worth about $12, from each departing
guest as he paid his bill. He used a behind-the-counter
adding machine to total the items in the bill, but quickly slid
the tape carriage aside while he punched an extra 100 pesos
into the machine. Ordinarily the guest paid the total shown

by the tape without question, and the cashier credited his account with the proper amount while pocketing the 100 pesos overpayment. But the scheme backfired when one guest, an accountant, added the tape. He handed it back to the embarrassed cashier with the suggestion that he re–add it—"without slipping the carriage." The cashier, of course, muttered that "the machine must have made a mistake,"

Facility in dealing with figures or quantitative concepts of course has a considerably loftier application than simply keeping bridge or golf scores or discovering errors in hotel bills. All economic activities are measured and expressed in quantitative terms. The accountant finds himself at home in these, not only because of his knowledge of accounting principles or auditing procedures, but because of his basic agility with numbers.

In fact, it is this special ability to assemble and analyze numbers and to perceive their meaning or significance that marks the expert accountant. For there is often a message buried in numbers that takes the accountant's special ability to uncover. Accounting has been likened to music. Both involve the interpretation of written symbols—in one case to determine economic condition or performance, and in the other, to produce sounds.

One accountant discovered a sizeable inventory valuation fraud late one night while doing simple arithmetic tests of a client's financial statements. Among other things, he computed various percentages and ratios and compared them to ascertain whether the figures made sense overall. They did not make sense, and, when he queried the company's controller the next morning about the disparate ratios, the controller admitted he had arbitrarily underpriced the inventory by almost $1 million to save taxes.

The value of the "sense test," by the way, is thoroughly acknowledged by experienced accountants. Some of the most blatant financial debacles of the 60s probably would not have occurred if someone had simply stood off from the detailed figures and made a common sense appraisal of the overall financial presentation. In one case, all of the alternative accounting principles selected for use in the company's financial reports apparently could have been defended, but the overall presentation was found grossly misleading.

Above and beyond the agility with figures that develops from constantly dealing with them, is the improvement that occurs in one's ability to analyze and deal with complex problems—all types of problems. Extensive experience with the behavior of numbers trains one to reason quantitatively. It sharpens one's logic and capacity to sift and evaluate all facets of a problem and to arrive at a rational, supportable decision. The non–trained person will say, "I think Alternative B is better." The accountant will ask, "How much better—10%, 40%, 80%?"—simply because he is trained to reason in quantitative terms.

All of which probably explains the presence of so many accounting–trained people at top management levels—like Thomas Murphy of General Motors and Harold Geneen of ITT. Both men started their careers working with numbers at rudimentary levels but gradually expanded their ways of thinking to ultimately deal with problems of world–wide proportions.

Preoccupation with figures and quantitative concepts, of course, can be overdone to the point that the more qualitative aspects of one's personality and one's normal relations with others suffer. Figures are so pure, so perfect, and so obedient, that they offer a seeming refuge from an otherwise imperfect world. There is such a thing as a figures addict—one who devotes all his time to dealing with numbers, to the virtual exclusion of everything else.

One New York inventory specialist, "a figurin' fool," worked 18 hours a day on clients' detailed inventory schedules, converting from the first–in, first–out method to the last–in, first–out method. The poor fellow so buried himself in thousands of figures that he shunned more wholesome human relationships altogether and became a recluse.

Every occupation has its zealots, but somehow the

"figures nut" is thought the most retarded. The musician who plays scales 18 hours a day is considered a potential artist. But no hope is held out for the figures nut. Probably because he deals with the purest of abstractions. Or because he is vaguely associated with the occasional gifted youngster who cannot tie his own shoelaces but can multiply four–digit numbers in his mind and rattle off the correct answer in seconds.

What's the point of all this? It's simply that, while accountants are adept with numbers, they also are heavily steeped in the environment in which the numbers reside. Figures, of course, are the basic tool and mode of expression in the economic world, and accountancy relies on the infinite forms and arrangements of the ten Arabic digits. But its substance is even broader. If one is to build a professional accounting practice, one should be intimately familiar with accountancy's broad environment and all its attributes and precepts. And he should be skilled in articulating these.

CONTRIBUTION TO CAPITAL MARKET DEVELOPMENT

Actually, accounting has been a major factor in the development of capital markets, in which massive funds are freely and efficiently accumulated, from widely dispersed sources, and put at the disposal of industry in general. The investment of this capital in plant and machines and in working funds has increased production and profits throughout the free world. Capital accumulation from widely dispersed sources is dependent upon reports of financial condition and results of operations—the credibility of which must not be in doubt. The accounting profession has supplied the credibility. It has done so by establishing a reputation for integrity, independence, and competence in the eyes of the millions of absentee capitalists, little and big, who must rely on published reports as a basis for their commitments. These number 25 million in the United States alone.

But reliance on the work of independent auditors does not stop with even these millions of shareholders. Banks and other institutional lenders, for example, look to a borrower's independent auditors for assurance that its financial condition is correctly portrayed in its statements, and that the various conditions of loan agreements have been met. Policyholders look to an insurance company's independent auditors for assurance that the company is financially viable and able to meet its future commitments. Outside directors depend on their company's independent auditors to help them discharge their responsibility for the accuracy of its financial presentations. Trustees of non-profit institutions look to their auditors to see that endowment and other special funds are properly used and accounted for.

Add to these the expectations of some 80 million American employees that independent auditors "keep management straight," and the countless customers and consumers who believe that the presence of independent auditors somehow reduces the chances of their being swindled.

The benefits implicit in independent financial auditing are universally acknowledged—practically every major enterprise is audited by professional accountants.

AUDITS AND PRODUCTIVITY

In addition to spurring capital investment, audits also inspire tighter controls and greater productivity within the enterprises themselves. It is well known, for example, that the Ford Motor Company sustained heavy losses while still privately–owned in the mid-forties, and that its outside auditors were unable to issue an unqualified audit report because of the absence of appropriate financial controls. When these were installed, a satisfactory audit not only became feasible, but the controls helped management ultimately achieve profitability for the company.

The value of the independent monitoring function has

also been demonstrated in hospitals, universities, and similar institutions. Most are audited by independent accountants, and while the audits focus on financial areas, they inspire firmer controls and improved productivity throughout.

Indeed, accountancy promotes general fiscal discipline and integrity and lends order to what might otherwise become a chaotic economic environment. One need look no further than to New York City during the summer of 1975 for the type of chaos that can stem from an absence of fiscal integrity and discipline. The city's virtual insolvency—its inability to finance ordinary operations, and, indeed, its astonishing ignorance of even the amount of its accumulated deficit—estimates ranged between $2.5 and $3.3 billion—precipitated ruinous strikes and work stoppages by sanitation workers, school teachers, policemen, and firemen. Ultimately the city's elected leaders were deposed for a time by a junta comprised principally of businessmen and state officials.

Large cities are beginning to follow industry's practice of engaging independent accountants to promote financial discipline and integrity in reporting and to enhance investor confidence in their securities.

In sum, without accountancy, today's far–flung economic institutions simply could not survive.

CHAPTER 7

Auditing's Changing Marketplace

A professional should be aware of the changing forces and trends in his profession—its history in perspective—if he is to understand its markets today. This is uniquely true of accountancy, which is based on ageless precepts.

Little that occurred before the Industrial Revolution, however, would hold much interest for the accountant. It simply is not relevant.

Except that the art of double entry bookkeeping was reportedly formalized by Fra Luca Pacioli in Italy in the late 15th Century, and it later gave rise to statements of financial condition and results of operations.

And accounting seems to have evolved almost sponteneously along the same general lines in most countries of the world, not because world communications were extensive, but because accounting apparently was a natural and logical response to the growing need for a methodology for recording the ownership of property and measuring the economic results of its use—all of which is sometimes referred to as the "accounting imperative."

Skilled bookkeepers had been on the scene for centuries, maintaining accounts and issuing statements for joint ventures and other enterprises. And "professional accountants" appeared as early as 1696 to oversee bankruptcies, liquidations, and receiverships under the Scottish Bankruptcy Act of that year.

PROFESSION SPAWNED IN UNITED KINGDOM

It was not until the 1850s that the independent, third-party expert accountant came on the scene. He was a product of the United Kingdom Companies Act of 1855, which introduced the limited liability company concept in order to attract outside capital and enable operations of scale.

That act stimulated a need for expert accounting counseling and systems work, as well as other "fiscal" services, including corporate secretaryships, trusteeships, and registration and transfer agents. Interestingly, accounting firms in the United Kingdom and on the Continent still perform these services, although they are customarily performed in the U.S. by banks.

The 1855 Companies Act and the 1862 Companies Act (the latter required registration of most U.K. companies for the first time) led to the formation of a great many companies in the United Kingdom operating on a large scale. They needed improved accounting methods and procedures to control operations that the expert accountant was able to supply.

Also, independent examinations of financial statements became more prevalent as the demand for assurances by outside shareholders and lenders mounted. Some of the world's most prestigious accounting firms originated in England at that time, including Price Waterhouse and Cooper Brothers.

The trend towards using third-party auditors was spurred by the Companies Act of 1879, which required independent audits of banks, and by the 1900 Act, which extended this requirement to *all* U.K. companies.

English financing of American railroads and steel companies in the 1870s and 1880s brought such firms as Barrow Wade & Guthrie, Price Waterhouse, and Peats to the U.S. Peats, of course, was the English wing of what is now Peat, Marwick, Mitchell & Co. In fact, Price Waterhouse and Peats formed several joint firms overseas in the early part of this century and operated until just recently in some South American and African countries as Price Waterhouse Peat & Co. Considering how competitive the two firms ultimately became in the United States, the Siamese Twins arrangement in those other countries must have been exasperating to both.

While industrial development in America was roughly 50 years behind that of Great Britain, individual American accountants nevertheless began to offer their services to the public as early as 1850. And when the English chartered accountants came on the American scene, professional standards began to emerge. The U.S. profession patterned itself after an experienced and already impressive English profession.

The American Association of Public Accountants was formed in 1887, and the first CPA laws were enacted in New York and Pennsylvania in 1896 and 1899 respectively. Several of the native American firms that are prominent today were founded then, including Haskins & Sells (1895) and Lybrand, Ross Bros. & Montgomery, now Coopers & Lybrand, (1898).

The U.S. accounting profession was on its way.

DEVELOPMENT OF AUDITING IN THE U.S.

There was no statutory requirement for independent audits of publicly held companies in the United States at the turn of the century. A few large companies, including United States Steel Corporation, voluntarily engaged outside auditors and issued their reports to the public. But since most companies were small, the public accountant was often just an adjunct to the accounting department of the business. He simply furnished the owner-manager with some assurance that the records were accurate and that the bookkeeper had not misappropriated any funds. Auditors were usually able to verify all or most transactions, and their report consisted of a notation in the records that they had been audited and found correct!

As businesses grew in size and complexity, however, it became increasingly impractical for auditor's to check all transactions. Therefore, they began to check or verify only selected blocks of transactions, such as cash receipts or disbursements for portions of the year.

Moreover, businesses increasingly resorted to outside

sources of capital, primarily banks and other credit grantors, to finance their growing needs. And these lenders came to rely on separately-bound, long-form auditors' reports for the monitoring of their commercial loans. A company's balance sheet was far more important to the creditors than its income statement, since they were primarily interested in liquidity. Accordingly, the reports tended to stress the balance sheet, and they included details or analyses of individual accounts as, for example, accounts receivable classified by age. Income statements, if included at all, were somewhat sketchy and indeed frequently omitted references to sales or revenues.

An important new "party-at-interest" was the American public, whose investment in industry was growing. As long as this investment was principally in bonds or other debt securities, management and auditors continued to stress the importance of the balance sheet. But when public ownership tended toward common stock and other equity securities, as it did in the 1920s, earning power became increasingly important, and the income statement achieved a stature commensurate with the balance sheet.

First Governmental Influence–1917

The Federal Reserve Board was the first government instrument to have a significant influence on audit procedures, auditors' reports, and financial statements. The Board, of course, had a natural interest in the credit worthiness of companies whose commercial paper was being discounted by Federal Reserve Banks. The auditing recommendations and statement forms contained in the Federal Reserve Bulletin of 1917 were almost universally adopted by the profession. And the recommendations and suggestions in the 1929 edition of the Federal Reserve Bulletin, entitled Verification of Financial Statements, formed the base for auditing procedures and statement presentations to this day.

The New York Stock Exchange also contributed to the development of acceptable accounting practices through its control over the financial reports issued by corporations listed on the exchange.

The organization of the Securities and Exchange Commission in 1933 to oversee the securities industry and to monitor financial reporting emphasized the persistently growing stake of the third-party securities holders. During this period, the standard short-form auditor's report attesting to the fairness of presentation of both financial condition and results of operations became universally used by publicly-held companies.

Also, during this period, the profession's standards and responsibilities in attesting to financial condition and the results of operations were reappraised and restated. Auditing procedures were adopted, for example, to uncover the type of fraud that had been perpetrated in the notorious McKesson-Robbins debacle of the late 1930s, where fake warehouse receipts were used to conceal a massive inventory shortage.

Auditing Techniques Restated—1939

Among other things, the 1939 reappraisal and restatement of auditing procedures sought to prescribe techniques that could be applied to almost any company in any industry. The system centered around balance sheet accounts which, except for variations in nomenclature or terminology, did not vary much among industries. That is, cash, receivables, inventories, and plant, for example, were treated the same, wherever in industry they were found or by whatever terms they were called. Auditing procedures focused mostly on the balance sheet accounts, and techniques were developed for verifying each of these. Thus receivables were to be confirmed by correspondence, inventories by physical observation, and so forth.

Income and expense accounts were not subjected to verification procedures as extensive as those used for balance sheet accounts, simply because the difference in net worth, reflected by the balance sheets at the beginning and end of the year, would in itself reflect a company's overall income or loss for the intervening period—after the effect of capital transactions and dividends had been eliminated.

Income statements, of course, could conceivably contain misclassifications of income or expense items, or might even cloak improper charges—for example, illegal payments or defalcations. But, since the avowed purpose of the examination was to enable the auditor to express an opinion on whether the statements *as a whole* fairly presented a company's financial condition at a certain date and the overall results of its operations for the year, minor misclassifications in income and expense were deemed immaterial.

Moreover, since, for reasons of economy, auditing procedures had to be limited to sampling and other tests, they could not uncover cleverly–concealed defalcations. The profession, therefore, sought to disclaim responsibility for uncovering relatively minor misappropriations, contending that internal auditing procedures and the bonding of employees should be relied upon for this protection. This was to be challenged later in the forum of public opinion.

Another new and important auditing concept that was adopted by the profession in the 1930s and 1940s was its reliance on the effectiveness of the client's system of internal control in determining the extent of verification needed for the accounts. Internal control systems had become increasingly prevalent over the years. Accordingly, a detailed review and evaluation of these controls, using questionnaires or checklists, became a normal auditing procedure, as did the practice of making tests of transactions to confirm the effectiveness of the controls. Ultimately, these reviews and tests were extended to include the new computer systems' controls.

This somewhat ingenious auditing system had achieved full maturity by the early 1950s, and, for a time, it met the needs of the financial and investment community for assurances about the financial condition and results of operations of publicly held companies.

But, apparently unknown to the profession, those needs were changing.

THE "LOOSE" ACCOUNTING PRINCIPLES

The improvements in auditing techniques were not accompanied by similar progress in accounting principles and reporting practices. The difference in the rate of development between the two is easy to understand. The profession had evolved the concept of "generally accepted accounting principles" and had adopted the practice of indicating the extent to which these principles had been adhered to in financial reports. The problem was that many laymen assumed that accounting principles, especially accounting principles that were supposedly "generally accepted," had been precisely defined when, in fact, to a great extent they were not even susceptible to exact definition.

Largely, accounting principles represented man-made, and admittedly arbitrary, conventions or customs that had been evolved through the years by economists and accountants to aid in measuring, reflecting, and communicating the results of economic activities. They were grounded on diverse theories that were reflected in numerous alternatives considered acceptable in any given area. Depreciation of physical plant, for example, could be viewed in many ways, all of which would produce different results from the others, but all of which would be considered acceptable. What was (and still is) lacking, of course, was a universal norm or standard of economic value—an illusive concept which, like beauty, is in the eye of the beholder. Although there are ways to express value, the most common being in dollars, the question of "how many" dollars depends on which theory or postulate is adopted in a given case.

Because the profession was aware of the diverse treatments that could be accorded a given economic condition or activity, and also that each treatment could attract rational support in theory, it was reluctant for years to even attempt to develop a set of rigid rules that would require similar transactions under similar conditions to be treated uniformly. Rather, it adopted broad postulates, such as the need for the periodic determination and reporting of earnings; the desirability of matching related income and expense items in the same period; and the concept of historical dollar cost. It fully recognized the many variations implicit within these postulates. But it relied, and indeed insisted, on consistency in the use of the particular treatment adopted by a given enterprise, so that the results reported in any given year would be reasonably comparable to those of the preceding year or years. The fact that different treatments of transactions could produce substantially different results and that earnings per share were not comparable among companies even within the same industry was, of course, recognized.

Attacks on Accounting Principles and Auditing Standards

In the late 1950s accounting principles and reporting practices came under attack from laymen and some accountants. These critics argued that the alternatives permitted were being exploited by business managements who tended to insist, understandably enough, on the use of principles that reflected the most favorable results for their companies. The critics also claimed that differences in the methods of computing earnings and earnings per share among various companies precluded meaningful comparisons. Greater exactitude was demanded. "Why, if we can land men on the moon at an exact place and time," they asked, "can we not determine precisely the exact earnings of a single business enterprise?" They urged greater uniformity in accounting principles.

In 1959 the American Institute of Certified Public Accountants organized the Accounting Principles Board to narrow the divergencies in accounting principles and reporting practices. The new board superceded the Committee on Accounting Procedures, which had been in existence since 1938. While the board ultimately issued some 31 formal opinions during the following 14 years, it was never able to shake off the suspicion that its members were beholden to corporate managements and were not completely objective or independent. Most of the members of the Board were practicing members of the profession from major firms.

Attacks on the Board began to undermine its credibility almost from the beginning and, as it turned out, these ultimately contributed to its demise in 1973, when it was replaced by the Financial Accounting Standards Board.

Actually, the profession was developing a serious "image" problem but apparently was not full aware of it.

The Suits Against Accountants—Growing Public Anxiety

Meanwhile, in the 1960s *auditing* procedures and disclosure practices had come under attack. This culminated in a rash of stockholder and creditor suits as well as criminal charges against a number of accountants and their firms for their alleged failure to discover or to report irregularities concerning companies whose statements they had examined. Those most highly publicized included *American Express, Yale Express, Westec, Barchris, Continental Vending Machine, National Student Marketing, Four Seasons Nursing Homes,* and *Equity Funding*—but there were many others.

The profession, through the AICPA's Auditing Procedures Committee, promptly undertook to repair the deficiencies in technical auditing procedures and reporting practices revealed by these cases. However, the publicity accorded the suits, following on the heels of the charges alleging "looseness" in accounting principles, no doubt increased the financial community's anxiety about the profession's standards generally, Public disillusionment was probably further aggravated by a belated awareness that most auditing standards and reporting practices were designed only to supply assurance that financial statements fairly reflect the overall financial condition and results of operations of the company—but no more than that.

By the middle 1960s, mutual funds and other large institutional investors had come to dominate the securities market, and the number of stockholders in publicly owned companies passed the 25 million mark. The division between ownership and management had become sharply drawn. Management had become "professional" and had greater influence on corporate fortunes than ever before. Its powers and prerogatives had increased. In the eyes of many, its responsibilities for the more effective use of capital and deployment of manpower had also increased.

Investors' appetites for more and better financial information were whetted; the highly sophisticated financial analysts in particular wished to evaluate management and operations more closely in order to better guide the fortunes of investors.

A single earnings-per-share figure was now found insufficient as a basis for making investment commitments. The emergence of conglomerates or diversified companies whose operations embraced multiple lines of business and whose income from a few profitable divisions could obscure unprofitability in others further weakened the value of the single figure. The demand by analysts for lines-of-business or segmentation reporting to enable a more detailed look at corporate activities inspired the Securities and Exchange commission in the early 1970s to require that this type of information be filed with it in certain cases.

The new Financial Accounting Standards Board, which succeeded the Accounting Principles Board in 1973 as the rule-maker on accounting principles and reporting practices, has had a similarly stormy existence. Although composed of non-practicing professionals who are insulated from client pressures, the Standards Board at the time of this writing is nevertheless under constant fire from both industry representatives and Congressional committees. See Metcalf Committee's Recommendations in Chapter 9, The U.S. Profession.

CHAPTER 8

The Special Services

SPECIAL ACCOUNTING SERVICES

The services of professional accountants are usually classified in three groups: auditing, tax services, and management consulting (or management advisory) services—auditing being considered the primary service and the others the special services. Actually, there are many special services within the auditing (and accounting) category. Some supplement the audit and others relate to SEC filings; still others are unique special assignments that accountants are qualified to undertake because of their skills in organizing and analyzing financial and economic information and data. The most unique assignments may involve such things as determining the estimated costs and economic feasibility of proposed public projects, which may range from a new state medical school to such giant undertakings as new port facilities, vast hydroelectric projects, or national transportation complexes—or evaluating the effectiveness of government spending programs. Every firm has its own list of unique assignments.

TAXES

Taxes have comprised an important part of accounting practice from before 1913. While many individual income tax returns and estate and inheritance tax returns are prepared by lawyers and others, business tax returns are prepared almost exclusively by accountants. This is because most business taxes are based on accounting concepts. The Federal corporation income tax, for example, is levied on "taxable

TABLE I—TYPES OF SPECIAL ACCOUNTING SERVICES

Supplemental Statements and Analyses

In connection with its primary function of examining and reporting upon clients' basic financial statements, accountants frequently furnish supplemental statements or analyses that are required by:

The Securities and Exchange Commission in initial registration statements and annual reports.

Banks or other credit grantors considering the extension of credit to the client.

Bankers or others concerned with bond indentures, loan agreements, preferred stock provisions and trust indentures.

Partnership agreements.

Institutional endowments and financing.

Prospective buyers or sellers of the business.

SEC Services

In additional to preparation and certification of financial statements for inclusion in SEC filings, accountants—

Advise lawyers and investment bankers on questions relating to the financial information required by the SEC.

Participate in pre-filing and post-filing conferences with SEC officials to resolve questions concerning financial information.

Review entire registration statements and related documents, including narrative sections.

Review indentures relating to proposed new issues of securities, underwriting agreements, and applications for listing on securities exchanges.

Issue conformity letters certifying that financial statements comply with SEC requirements.

Issue "comfort letters" to underwriters indicating that the accountants' reviews of unaudited interim financial statements had revealed nothing that would dispute the fairness of the overall presentations.

Issue letters regarding adverse changes in the companies' financial positions and the results of their operations during unaudited interim periods.

Issue letters furnishing specified financial data, such as analyses of sales by products, departments or lines of business; renumeration; and fixed asset additions and retirements for a period of years.

Special Assignments

Accountants also frequently undertake special assignments that are not related to annual audits. Some of the traditional examples are:

Reporting on compliance with indentures or similar agreements.

TABLE I—TYPES OF SPECIAL ACCOUNTING SERVICES *(continued)*

Preparing or reviewing renegotiation data.

Verifying rentals or royalties based on volume of business.

Investigating businesses to be acquired.

Assembling data and formulating plans for sales, mergers, or dissolutions.

Determining amounts under incentive compensation plans.

Preparing data in support of insurance losses.

Investigating defalcations.

Reviewing accounting provisions of proposed contracts, incentive compensation plans, pension plans, partnership agreements, and corporate reorganizations.

Testifying as expert witnesses.

Reviewing interim financial statements.

---

income." Such accounting concepts as sales, costs, inventories and depreciation are involved in determining taxable income.

Similarly, the three wartime excess profits taxes in 1917, 1941, and 1950 were levied on a portion of corporate profits that exceeded a stipulated norm. The determination of profits that were deemed "excess" were also based on fundamental elements of accounting such as invested capital, average earnings, and average rates of return.

Also, corporation taxes levied by most states are based on accounting concepts. Usually they are levied on some portion of the company's net income or net assets that is apportioned to the respective state by arithmetic formula.

The sources of the accounting elements necessary to compute both Federal and State corporation taxes are the income and surplus accounts, and the balance sheets of corporate taxpayers. These, in turn, are developed from information obtained from the financial books and records of the corporation.

Because the accountant had accumulated the necessary accounting and factual data from his clients' records in connection with his audits, business largely turned to him to prepare its first returns upon the enactment of the 1909 and 1913 Federal income tax laws. He followed up the preparation of returns by defending their accuracy upon examination by Internal Revenue agents, and he protested proposed deficiencies before the Conference Sections. He prepared claims for refund of overpaid taxes and sought and obtained rulings from the Treasury concerning the tax effects of completed or prospective transactions.

As tax law, both statutory and judicial, became more complex over the years, specialization developed in taxation. Even in moderate sized accounting firms at least one accountant is assigned to full time specialization in tax matters. These specialists evolved not only because of the volume and complexity of the tax work itself, but because determining accurate provisions for taxes in certified financial statements require an expert and intimate knowledge of tax procedure.

The Lawyer–CPA Dispute

In 1935 the Unauthorized Practice of Law Committee of the American Bar Association expressed concern over the extent to which "accountants and other laymen" were engaged in filling out income tax returns and were enrolled to practice before the Treasury. The committee took the position that certain activities, such as preparing protests against proposed tax deficiencies, constituted the practice of law, and should be performed by lawyers. It recommended that the public be advised that the services of lawyers should be enlisted in this field of work—and it urged that lawyers be given more opportunity to gain knowledge of the law of taxation so as to be better qualified to render public service in the tax field.

In the 1940s suits were brought by several local bar associations against accountants—including a New York certified public accountant, one Bernard Bercu—seeking to enjoin them from certain aspects of tax practice. In general, the decisions went against the accountants. Concurrently the rules of practice of several governmental administrative tribunals were tightened against the admission of accountants. And Congress itself got into the question of administrative practice during the enactment of a new administrative procedure act in 1946.

Meanwhile, representatives of the American Bar Association and the American Institute of CPAs strove to reach agreement on the respective roles of the two professions in tax practice and succeeded in bringing about a spirit of voluntary cooperation between their members.

But the dispute was not finally laid to rest until 1954, when Secretary George Humphrey announced that the Treasury would continue to admit CPAs to practice, and he urged a continuing live–and–let–live attitude between the two professions. And while there is still considerable overlapping in the services rendered by the two professions in the field of taxes, they have been at peace ever since.

ENTRANCE INTO MANAGEMENT CONSULTING

Auditors installed accounting systems and advised clients on financial and operating matters virtually from the beginning. This competence stemmed from the auditors' basic contact with management methods and business operations—just as their tax competence had stemmed from experience with statute ordained accounting concepts.

There was a period in the teens when some leaders of the profession apparently considered management services potentially incompatible with auditing independence, on the grounds that the auditor engaged in consulting might be deemed to be auditing his own work. The formation in 1919 of the National Association of Cost Accountants (now the National Association of Accountants) apparently was to furnish "housing" for the non–auditor sector of the accounting profession. And for several decades thereafter, most consulting work was performed by management consulting firms or others.

The large accounting firms formally entered management consulting in the late 1940s or early 1950s, inspired, no doubt, by marketplace demands. Consulting had not achieved an independent professional status. There was no defined body of knowledge or standard of competence, nor was there control over the qualifications of those who held themselves out as management consultants. And, while individual firms of undoubted integrity and competence existed, the public was not generally protected from unqualified practitioners.

Accountancy, on the other hand, had gained recognition as a disciplined profession and enjoyed the confidence of the business community. Accounting firms, therefore, undertook to fill a consulting void.

Naturally, accounting firms tended to stress the types of consulting services they were most familiar with, such "quantitative" areas as financial and budgetary control systems, management information systems, electronic computer systems and controls, manufacturing control systems, and sales, marketing, and profitability analyses. Some firms, however, went further and entered such fields as operations research, executive recruiting, and actuarial.

A Philosophic Conflict Between Consulting and Auditing?

The SEC and others have intermittently expressed concern that furnishing consulting services to auditing clients might impair an accounting firm's objectivity and independence and result in substandard financial reporting, which in turn could erode investor and lender confidence. At the time of this writing there has even been some thought, voiced particularly by several Congressional Committees, that auditing should retreat to a separate and quasi–judicial sort of function, with the consulting functions to be abandoned to find other housing—possibly with law firms or management consulting firms. (See the Metcalf Committee's Rcommendations in Chapter 9, The U. S. Profession.)

Auditing, of course, is the traditional discipline, and the most distinctive one. It distinguishes accountancy from other professions or occupations. Tax consulting can be, and frequently is, performed by lawyers and others, and management consulting by consulting firms and others. But only the accounting profession performs auditing for third-party assurance.

And of the three disciplines, only auditing is deemed to be vested with the concept of complete independence. This is not considered basic to the consulting disciplines. Indeed, advocacy is probably more appropriate in tax consulting.

In retrospect, the several disciplines came to be handled by accountants because of their technical affinity, and because they deal with similar, if not identical, subject matter. But of even greater significance is the indication from the profession's history that it was the marketplace itself that recognized this technical affinity, and, having a genuine, tangible need, it was simply not interested in any conceptual or philosophic problems that the profession may have had.

Also, the conceptual differences between auditing and the consulting services are probably not as wide as they may seem. Audit objectivity and independence are not necessarily weakened by tax consulting, for example. There does not seem to be any reason why an accountant of integrity cannot push for a favorable construction of an ambiguous tax regulation while representing his client in government proceedings and, at the same time, insist upon a higher, more conservative provision for the disputed tax in the client's financial statements. Neither the advocacy of consulting nor the independence of auditing suffers. There is no basic conflict of interest in such cases and, so far as is known, none has been successfully asserted during the 65 years that the profession has been engaged in tax practice. Moreover, the now prevalent use of experienced tax personnel in verifying tax provisions or accruals in connection with the examination of financial statements surely enhances the quality of the statements.

Nor do management consulting services present any substantially different implications. The technical affinity has always been present here, too, as has the commonality of the subject matter.

Indeed, management services expertise should enable accountants to better report on the operational aspects of the businesses and institutions they audit—a practice that would not only serve the growing information needs of mounting absentee owners, but would also add to the productivity and profitability of the organizations themselves. Unfortunately, the profession has just scratched the surface of using consultants' help in auditing.

The ultimate question, of course, is whether these several competencies, as increasingly integrated functions in a single profession, can lend more order to our economic institutions. If the answer is in the affirmative, and it would seem that the marketplace has already decided this, the profession undoubtedly should continue to pursue the broader role, in order to respond to the needs of the economy in the future.

If, on the other hand, the accounting profession's auditing credibility is to genuinely suffer because of the presence of the several consulting competencies, the public interest would seem to dictate that consulting services be abandoned in favor of auditing.

But what a pity that would be!

CHAPTER 9

The U. S. Profession

After interviewing the chairman of the Accounting Principles Board for over an hour, the writer from the prominent business magazine gathered his notes, rose, thanked his subject, and left.

On the way out he complained to the chairman's associate, "As far as I'm concerned, that (interview) was a total loss. Here he is, the managing partner of a big accounting firm and chairman of an important rule–making body—yet all he talks about is accounting rulings."

"I gave him every opportunity to expound on important matters like accountancy's contribution to industry productivity and capital markets, and its role in restoring credibility to government, and that sort of thing," he said, "yet he kept returning to APB 15 and 16 or some other accounting rule. I would think a man in his position would have more breadth and vision—greater imagination than that." "I simply do not have a story," he concluded.

"I think you *do* have a story," the chairman's associate replied. "It's a fairly simple story, a down to earth story, a genuine story."

"Accounting is not especially romantic," the associate went on. "It's a social science, that expresses itself in numbers. And auditing is a methodical, demanding discipline. It requires infinite commitment and concentration to carry it out effectively."

"Nor are auditors inclined to be flamboyant or expansive," the associate observed. "They're certainly not the charismatic executives or colorful tycoons you are apt to find in other industries. And they are not as expressive as, say, their tax colleagues, whose work demands assertiveness . . . Rather, they are essentially conservative, modest people."

"The man you just interviewed," the associate continued, "is an auditor—in fact he is one of the world's outstanding auditors. He is regarded as a top authority on auditing; he wrote one of the pivotal books."

"Now if you were asked to select someone to take charge of building a body of accounting rules," the associate asked, "a task that requires high technical ability and a step by step, structured approach, whom would you pick—one of the more vociferous critics of accountancy, or this methodical man?"

"I get the story" the writer said as he went out the door. And his story, which concentrated on the almost ingenuous simplicity of one representative accountant, managed to convey the essence of the auditing profession—a fierce dedication to accounting and auditing theory and practice.

Profession Built Around Auditing. The fact is that the profession is built around the attest function, auditing. Auditing accounts for some 70% of the work of the major firms, with tax and management advisory services averaging but 15% each. As pointed out in Chapter 8, The Special Services, auditing is the most distinctive discipline—the one that distinguishes accountancy from all other professions. Only the accounting profession performs auditing for third party assurance.

Auditing's socio-economic impact is infinitely more extensive than that of tax services or management advisory services. Indeed, the ultimate impact of the latter pale alongside that of auditing. Moreover, auditing is invested with more exacting moral and philosophic precepts than the other functions.

As a result, the audit function is viewed as pivotal in all the large accounting firms, with the responsibility for all services rendered the client resting finally with the audit partner. The audit partners bring in the bulk of the fees, and they hold all the trump cards in the management of the large accounting firm.

Of course, the profession is more than 50% comprised of local CPA partnerships and one–man firms whose revenues are principally derived from worthwhile and badly needed write–up services (bookkeeping), as well as the preparation of unaudited financial statements and tax services.

But this does not dilute the all–pervasive importance of auditing in the profession. Indeed, the auditing mystique is primarily responsible for the unique organizational form of large accounting firms—a phenomenon that evokes great interest in outsiders, most of whom associate organizational bigness exclusively with large, publicly owned corporations.

UNIQUE STRUCTURING OF ACCOUNTING FIRMS

A large accounting firm has unique organizational characteristics. It must recognize the personal and individual nature of professional accountability and legal liability—the CPA's responsibility to anyone who relies on his reports. And it must provide sufficient latitude for the individual accountant to exercise his professional prerogatives and judgment within the framework of his firm's overall standard of quality.

But the accounting firm is also a functioning economic organism. The traditional trappings of good organization must be installed if it is to operate efficiently and profitably while still maintaining uniform and consistent practice standards. Both good operating policies and technical standards must be adhered to throughout the firm.

Therefore, while accounting firms are traditionally partnerships, the larger firms are organized and operated like corporations. They have a well–conceived plan of formal organization and carefully evolved definitions of position and authority, as well as a clear outline of everyone's duties and responsibilities. These are precisely set forth in appropriate policy, administrative, and operating manuals. To be effective, the plan of organization must promote administrative and economic efficiency on the one hand, but not be so stringent as to constrict individual freedom or professional incentive on the other.

Until recently, state law, as well as AICPA policy, prevented the incorporation of accounting firms, although this has been relaxed of late. The AICPA and some states now permit professional organizations to incorporate without limiting their liability with respect to professional services. But until all states adopt a professional incorporation provision, the national accounting firms are not likely to incorporate.

All the major firms have the traditional line-and-staff type of organization. Their partners and principals can be viewed in a corporate sense as the "stockholders." A distinction is made between partners and principals, however, because a firm cannot represent itself to the public as "certified public accountants" unless all its partners are CPAs. The partners of the various firms, then, are its legal owners.

Principals, while often highly qualified members of other professions, are not CPAs and therefore cannot legally be owners. But from an operating viewpoint they often have the same stature, authority, and responsibilities as partners.

The "charter" of a partnership, which is analogous to a corporation's charter, is a partnership contract that binds all partners and principals. It usually assigns operational and administrative responsibilities to a management or executive committee elected by the partners and headed by the managing partner or chairman. The executive committee is usually empowered to establish the shares of all the partners in the net income of the firm. These are changed from time to time, usually upward as the partner's prestige and value to the firm increases.

The source of the firm's capital is the partners themselves, although most firms supplement their short term working capital with intermittent bank borrowings. Typically, the partners' capital accounts are built up over an extended period by the firm's withholding a specified percentage, say 15%, of the partners' share of annual income until an agreed upon amount of capital is accumulated. This is returned to the partner on his retirement or withdrawal from the firm. Firms also provide retirement benefits or pensions to partners as well as employees.

The typical staff organization of a firm, as contrasted with its "line" organization, is composed of partners who head up the several areas of technical practice—auditing, tax services, management advisory services, and international services, as well as partners or other top persons who head up such administrative functions as finance, personnel, training, and development.

The firm's line or operating organization is comprised of local practice offices, each of which has its own managing partner or partner in charge and staffs of auditors, tax people, and consultants. The operating organization is usually divided into geographic regions or divisions, dependiing on the size of the firm and the dispersion of offices.

The major accounting firms are considerably better organized today than, say, 30 years ago, when it was felt that the surrender of the partners' individual prerogatives would stifle professional incentive. But there were other reasons for the marked improvement in accounting organizations. Even the large firms were somewhat monolithic, in that some were still headed by one of the venerable pioneers of the profession—usually a powerful super–leader. Such names as Robert Montgomery, Arthur Young, George O. May, and Arthur Andersen come to mind. In most cases the head man proclaimed policy and made the important decisions, in what was less than a democratic process. There was no need for any other governing apparatus. But as these giants departed from the scene without leaving similarly positioned successors, they had to be replaced by the blocks and lines of an organization chart. Indeed, some firms were reported to have drafted definitive organization charts in the 1950s for the first time.

Another reason for formalizing firm organizations was to provide a framework for expansion and growth. The special services departments were growing in stature and pushing for recognition. What had been a Director of Practice then became three directors—Director of Accounting and Auditing, Director of Tax Services, and Director of Management Services—and the assimilation of the many new partners from merged firms called for formal charts and manuals to define their role and responsibilities. (See "The Merger Wave" in Chapter 13.)

Still another reason for strengthening firm organizations was the recognition that accountancy should gear up for its increasing importance in the socio-economic world. The economy was developing into a number of separate and massive societies—industry, government, the universities, the military, the labor union, and others. Their monitoring and control requirements were critical. Accountancy was seen as the key to ordering these vast organizations, and thus accountants became infused with a sense of mission. One–generation confederations of independent practitioners were not adequate to discharge the expanded role. Succession, continuity, and even perpetuity had to be provided to the most humanly possible extent. Firms had to be structured to last far into the future.

Fortunately, accountants had not only the mentality for structuring strong organizations and operating them efficiently; they also had a common philosophic objective— truth, the governing ethic of the profession.

It is interesting to compare the major accounting firms and their philosophic objective with the Church and its spiritual objective, and to conjecture about the future role of accountancy. Is it possible, for example, that events are conspiring to catapult the accounting profession into the position of principal monitors of world economic order? This could be—though no one would be more surprised than accountants themselves, or more reluctant to assume the exalted position of keeper of the economic ethic.

Accountancy's future role depends on the extent to which it can reestablish public confidence in its integrity and rid itself of the threat of inordinate governmental intervention. A profound public relations challenge!

THE PUBLIC CONFIDENCE IMPERATIVE

The credibility that accountants add to financial reports upon which investors and lenders rely in making their commitments depends upon the confidence of the public in their character and integrity. Without this trust the role of accountants would be no more than that of technicians.

Accordingly, the entire history of the profession has been marked by continuous efforts to develop and preserve integrity, character, and an acute sense of responsibility in its members. And the profession's success in this perpetual moral indoctrination was no doubt responsible for the public confidence it enjoyed during most of its years. The auditor's attestation to the fairness of financial presentations was generally accepted as assurance that all was well.

This confidence probably began to erode in the 1960s with the highly publicized attacks on alleged deficiencies in accounting principles and auditing procedures. It receded further with the torrent of suits against accountants and their firms in the late 1960s and early 1970s, when scarcely a week went by without an accounting "horror story" appearing in the press. Not only was the profession's technical competence challenged, but its basic moral character and integrity were questioned as well. Accountants were accused of laxity, prostituting their professional skills, and conspiring with management. Several accountants were convicted in criminal proceedings brought under securities acts.

After reading about a particularly flagrant case in the New York Times one morning, a friend remarked on the train platform, "It sounds to me as though your profession is made up of a bunch of crooks"—a little extreme, perhaps, but indicative of a common tendency to condemn an entire society for the actions of a few.

At some stage the leaders of the profession had to seriously question whether the profession could recover from these devastating attacks—whether it could rebuild its credibility and resume its role in lending order to man's economic activities, particularly his pursuits under the highly developed industrial complex that exists today. These activities, of course, cannot be conducted without adherence to order any more than heavy automobile traffic can be controlled without ordnances or lights. That order requires a monitorship that is not only technically superior and alert, but also possessed of such loftier attributes as objectivity, integrity, moral courage, and a personal sense of responsibility.

Actually, there was no other profession, group, or calling that had both the technical abilities and the philosophic base needed to meet the demands of the increasingly complex multinational industrial society. Certainly not the United States government, or one of the other professions, or indeed even one of those traditional monitors of morality, the church and the universities. Aside from lacking the required technical knowledge, all had developed credibility problems of their own, as cynicism ate away at accepted social standards. Moreover, despite the cloud on the accounting profession's image, it was apparent that the public continued to look to it to keep order, and to be the monitor of the business ethic.

Actually, accountants have always tried to be rugged individualists and undoubtedly have succeeded 99% of the time. But moral courage is not a constant quality. It surges and recedes between generations and, indeed, within the lifetime or even a day of a single person. Someone has observed that we are considerably less courageous at night than at high noon—that we are all cowards at 4 A. M.

The confrontation with truth, when it occurs, is always a personal and solitary experience. Every accountant experiences such confrontations repeatedly during his career. Indeed, an active member of the profession encounters more potential moral confrontations in a year than the average person does in a lifetime.

The accountant may be pushed to reflect a transaction or a condition improperly in a financial report or to color a tax report in order to cover up for management or to make the company look better.

He may be pressed to help formulate a policy or position against the public interest. Members of the Financial Accounting Standards Board, for example, are wrestling with broad problems right now, as they seek to eliminate poor accounting and reporting practices in the face of intense pressures by those who want them left alone.

Or, in a more subtle form, the confrontation may be reflected in persuasion from within the accountant's own organization, even from a colleague or superior, who in all good faith urges him to take a position contrary to his own convictions.

Most accountants try not to bear these burdens alone. They are encouraged to and do seek advice and counsel from their associates. But it is both a moral and legal credo that professional accountants are individually responsible for the exercise of judgment in discharging their duties. The auditor is personally responsible for any professional work he undertakes. So is the tax man and the consultant, when they are dealing with engagements in their particular areas of competence. This often requires the taking of a personal position against strong and threatening opposition in what must be the most classic form of moral confrontation in modern society.

Once in a while an accountant may yield to the pressure—and aid or abet an impropriety, if not an outright crime. But 99% of the time the accountant stands firm—based on the author's observations during his many years of practice. The trouble, from the viewpoint of the profession's image, is that the public hears of an occasional dereliction or weakess sometimes through a highly publicized charge or suit. It practically *never* hears of the thousands of instances when accountants have heroically put their convictions on the line—and stayed with them.

The profession has never relaxed its dedication to high moral standards. It has always encouraged its young members to get into the habit early of facing up to their problems. For, after the first instance, facing the later ones becomes easier. As he becomes known as a person of principle, the accountant invariably finds that the confrontations all but disappear, as those who would bend him to their wishes come to realize that any such effort would be futile. Invariably he inspires greater respect for himself and his firm—and indeed the entire profession.

Less than 2% of the suits against accountants have charged moral lapse. The great majority involved technical aberrations—inadequate procedures or simple bungling. *This* is the area the profession is concentrating on at the time of this writing. And it is making significant progress in shoring up auditing procedures and standards and improving staff training programs. It is endeavoring to satisfy public expectations and reestablish its credibility.

THE METCALF COMMITTEE'S RECOMMENDATIONS

The most extensive Congressional inquiry into the accounting profession and the auditing of publicly owned companies since the 1930s was conducted in the years 1975–1977 by the Subcommittee on Reports, Accounting and Management of the Senate Committee on Governmental Affairs. Chaired by the late Senator Lee Metcalf and popularly referred to as the Metcalf Committee, the subcommittee issued its recommendations in late 1977. They are bound to have a far reaching and generally salutary effect on auditing and reporting standards and professional accounting practice.

Establish Self-Regulatory Organization of Firms. The subcommittee urged the establishment of a self–regulatory organization of accounting firms that audit publicly owned companies, with disciplinary powers similar to those of the New York Stock Exchange and the National Association of Securities Dealers. The firms would be required to submit to regular peer reviews; to periodically rotate audit partners on SEC engagements; to require staff members to take continuing professional education courses; to publish organizational, financial, and operating data annually; and to meet other performance and behavior standards.

Limit Types of Management Services. The subcommittee recommended that independent auditors of publicly owned companies perform only those types of management services that are directly related to accounting, and discontinue such non–accounting services as "executive recruitment, marketing analysis, plant layout, product analysis, and actuarial."

Relax Artificial Bans on Advertising and Promotion. The subcommittee also recommended the removal of artificial restrictions against advertising and talking with another firms's clients or employees, in order to enable small firms, particularly, to inform existing and potential clients of their abilities. The subcommittee urged "competition in pricing and innovation balanced by a strong program to assure that professionalism and independence are not compromised."

Require Formation of Corporate Audit Committees. Finally, the subcommittee recommended that the accounting profession or the SEC require that publicly held corporations establish audit committees comprised of outside directors as a a condition for being accepted as a client by an independent auditor. Audit committee members, according to the subcommittee, should be free of any significant involvement with the management of a corporation, including commercial or investment relationships, outside legal counsel, management consulting, or major commercial relationships.

Purpose and Duties of the Audit Committee. According to the subcommittee:

> The major purpose of the corporate audit committee should be to handle relations with the independent auditor, improve internal auditing controls, and establish appropriate policies to prohibit unethical, questionable or illegal activities by corporate em-

ployees. An audit committee should have sole authority to hire the independent auditor, set the audit fee, and dismiss the auditor. In addition, the audit committee should meet privately with the independent auditor, receive full reports from the auditing firm on its findings and be informed of all services being provided to the corporation by the auditing firm. The audit committee's own independence could perhaps be increased by rotating its chairman.

Independent auditors should use their expertise to help audit committees establish strong internal auditing controls and high standards of conduct for corporate employees. Compliance with those standards and controls should be reviewed as part of the independent audit, and the auditor's report to the public should comment on the adequacy of the standards and controls, as well as compliance with them.

The subcommittee also recommended that the audit committees review the propriety of special perquisites enjoyed by senior management, including special housing, personal loans, club memberships, and personal travel and pleasure—and that the independent auditors should monitor these "perks."

The American Institute of Certified Public Accountants acted immediately upon the recommendations of the subcommittee by establishing a new self–regulatory organization of firms known as the SEC Practice Section of the AICPA Division of CPA Firms. Its charter reflects most of the subcommittee's recommendations. The Institute also has modified the rules of conduct on advertising and solicitation— and no doubt some action on the audit committee recommendation will take place in the near future.

A FEW STATISTICS

There are approximately 185,000 certified public accountants in the United States at the time of this writing (December 1977). Of these, 134,000 are members of the American Institute of Certified Public Accountants.

The Institute reports that 58% of its members are engaged in public accounting practice, with 36% employed in business or industry, and 3% each in education and government.

The Institute stratifies its some 77,000 members who are in public accounting practice as follows:

Firms with one AICPA member	22%
Firms with 2 to 9 members	30
Firms with 10 or more members (except the 25 largest firms)	12
25 largest firms	36

There apparently are no similar breakdowns available for the some 51,000 CPAs who are not members of the American Institute. One can only deduce that of the 185,000 *total* CPAs in the United States, roughly 100,000 are engaged in public practice—give or take 10,000.

The twenty-five largest firms include the so–called Big Eight international firms, some six national firms, and eleven of nineteen regional firms.

According to *Who Audits America,* the 25 largest firms audit over 80% of the 8,077 publicly held companies and over 95% of their total sales. The Big Eight firms alone account for 71% of the total number of companies and 94% of their total sales.

The Accounting Profession, a superbly researched 200 page book by John W. Buckley and Marlene H. Buckley, is a complete factual and informative description of accountancy. It contains 61 exhibits and four useful appendices. Published in 1974 by Melville Publishing Company, it is recommended without qualifications to anyone interested in pursuing the anatomy of accountancy in some depth.

CHAPTER 10

U.S. Accounting Goes International

The extensive overseas expansion of American accounting firms in the 1950s and 1960s was inevitable. The American firms simply followed their clients' burgeoning investments abroad just as the English firms had followed their clients' investments overseas some 75 years before.

Although England had been the world's largest export-er of capital for more than a century prior to World War I, the United States clearly overtook the U. K. after World War II. Then, many American companies that previously had had relatively little interest in foreign operations stepped up their overseas commitments in order to cash in on the im-proved and bigger world markets that arose from the miraculous reconstruction of Europe, the stabilizing of gov-ernments and currencies, and the formation of extra–national economic communities.

AMERICANS' IMMERSION IN OVERSEAS ACCOUNTING

American accountants, however, were not as knowledgeable or as sophisticated in international trade or business as the English Chartered Accountants. They simply had not had the same exposure. America had been a net capital importer almost until World War I. It had been immersed in develop-ing its own industries and infrastructure. Indeed, American foreign policy had long discouraged overseas involvement, or "foreign entanglements," as it was called. And the coun-try's brief involvement in World War I simply reinforced its determination to remain neutral—whatever might develop abroad. This insularity, of course, ended abruptly in 1941 with the attack on Pearl Harbor, and America then became an active participant in the world community.

England, on the other hand, had long been a predominant international power. The U.K.'s economy was built around commerce with the many countries and territories that comprised the Empire, as well as with other trading nations. At the height of his country's influence, one English statesman reportedly observed, "Britain has neither permanent friends nor permanent enemies—only permanent interests."

In such an environment the English chartered accountant was literally weaned on international trade and investment and foreign service from the time he was a schoolboy. And though the profession fanned out to India, Australia, New Zealand, Rhodesia, and the many other British–linked nations during the late 1800s, the chartered accountant continued to look to the U.K. as his professional home. The English profession and the Institute of Chartered Accountants of England and Wales exerted the single greatest influence on world accounting for three quarters of a century. Other "international" professions had also developed in such countries as Germany and The Netherlands, but none approached the English in stature or influence.

Despite their late arrival on the international scene, American accountants lost no time in immersing themselves in international accounting. They not only migrated abroad in large numbers after World War II—they seized the initiative in identifying and cataloging differences in foreign accounting principles and reporting practices as a first step towards ultimately "harmonizing" world accounting.

In response to the pleas from delegates to the International Accounting Congress in New York in 1962, the AICPA's Committee on International Relations undertook a comprehensive study of world accounting. Its findings were published in the 600–page *Professional Accounting in 25 Countries* and summarized in a 1965 *Journal of Accountancy* article entitled "Some Observations on World Accounting."

The Insititute Committee's findings stimulated interest in many countries and apparently spurred constructive action in some whose standards were low. Robert Olivetti, then head of the Olivetti Typewriter Company, was particularly curious to learn from the author who directed the study, how the committee found accounting standards in Italy.

"Surely you must already know how we found Italian Accounting and reporting standards," the author stated during a visit to Mr. Olivetti's office. "There is a dearth of reliable financial information available concerning Italian companies. Everything seems quite secretive."

"Ah yes," replied Mr. Olivetti, who had attended the Harvard Graduate School of Business. "It is, of course, Italy's tax system that compels this secrecy. Taxpayer compliance in our country is somewhat loose, and has been for generations. While our tax rates are set high enough to offset the traditional under–reporting of income, Italian companies obviously cannot report one amount of income to the tax authorities and another to the public."

Mr. Olivetti went on to observe that little could be done to improve disclosure standards until tax reform was effected. "And that will take a long time," he added.

However other countries, including France, Germany, and Brazil, immediately instituted improvements in their reporting standards, bringing them closer to those of the U. S. and the U. K.

Formalizing International Accounting Standards

A formal effort to harmonize and perhaps even codify accounting principles and reporting practices for international use began with the formation in 1973 of the International Accounting Standards Committee, an extra–national group composed of representatives from 40 countries. At the time of this writing, the Committee has adopted seven standards and issued exposure drafts for nine others. Acceptance of its recommendations within all countries will undoubtedly be slow, but this should not impede international trade or investment significantly, since the intercompany reports on foreign operations of at least the large international companies are usually adjusted anyway to conform with the practices prevailing in the headquarters country.

As a result of its immersion in international accounting, the American profession has taken its place alongside the English as a major influence in world accounting. This lofty position now shared by the two professions is, of course, a by–product of history. For while accountants help keep history going, they cannot be said to be prime movers or innovators. Their work no doubt contributed to capital development in many countries, but the profession certainly did not originate the capital. Others did. And if it can be said that a competent and respected accounting profession goes hand in hand with the existence of capital markets, the English and American professions would seem to owe their relative affluence as much to the economic and financial vigor of their respective countries as the converse.

METHODS OF FOREIGN EXPANSION BY AMERICAN FIRMS

Methods of foreign expansion by American accounting firms during the 1950s were influenced largely by the status of accountancy in the foreign country or countries into which they moved. That is to say, the nature, the stature, and the standards of the accounting profession, if any, that already existed in the particular foreign country and the local laws governing accounting practice, were highly influential.

Where a capable profession existed in a foreign country and reputable local firms of high standards were there, the American firms tended to become associated with those firms. Countries where this occurred included the United Kingdom and the British–linked nations, where there was a highly developed profession and very high standards of accounting and financial reporting. The same was true of

Canada, where the accounting profession compared almost exactly in methods and standards with the American profession. And there were fine professions and well established firms in Germany, Switzerland, and Scandinavia.

So a U. S. firm like Haskins & Sells simply strengthened its longstanding relationship with the venerable English firm of Deloitte, Plender & Griffiths. Indeed, the composite name of Deloitte, Haskins & Sells was adopted worldwide in early 1978. And Ernst & Ernst strengthened its relationship with Whinney Smith & Whinney (now Whinney Murray & Co.), which had long operated in the United Kingdom and in some Continental countries. Also, Arthur Young & Co. and Touche entered into close arrangements with the large Canadian firms of Clarkson & Gordon and P. S. Ross, respectively. And Lybrand joined with Cooper Brothers of the U. K. and McDonald, Currie & Company of Canada to form Coopers & Lybrand.

In many other countries, however, the method of expansion had to be somewhat different—simply because of the lower standards of accounting, financial reporting, and, indeed, of the accounting professions, if any. This was particularly true in most of the South American countries. Argentina, though, was an exception. It had had a relatively progressive profession since around 1910. It had had an active stock exchange and a securities law that governed the standards of financial reporting. Therefore, its accounting firms were relatively more mature than those in other South American Countries. But in practically all the other South American Countries North American personnel simply had to be imported and native personnel educated, trained, and developed almost from scratch.

Finally, there were a few countries in the world with highly developed accounting professions, but with local laws that prohibited their associating with outside firms—for example, the Philippines. American firms have not been able to establish themselves there. Clients of the American firms have simply had to utilize the local firms in the Philippines.

Multinational Form of Organization

In the process of foreign expansion the American firms tended mostly towards multinational types of organizations comprised of member firms that originated in their respective world areas. Most of the member firms are partnerships, as in the case of U. S. and U. K. firms. But German or Swiss member firms are usually incorporated, since accounting firms have traditionally taken the corporate form in those countries.

The international firms, then, are generally super-partnerships of member forms operating under a common name. Their charters provide for an appropriate governing body, and they define its scope and authority as well as the rights, interests and responsibilities of the various member firms. The need to maintain consistent practice standards in all countries is recognized by all the international firms, and this is usually accomplished through international manuals and other technical memoranda, with the work continuously monitored by international liaison groups or committees.

While some of the international firms undoubtedly went through a loose confederation stage in the beginning, most have become unified organisms and operate quite smoothly in hundreds of cities world-wide.

PART III

ACCOUNTANCY'S MARKETS AND ITS PUBLICS

CHAPTER 11

The Industry Markets

The market for accounting services need not be viewed as a myriad of faceless entities, but rather as a matrix of unique industries having special attributes and characteristics, all of which call for differing approaches to the types of professional accounting services they require.

For accountancy's purposes, this industry universe can be classified into ten giant divisions (e.g., construction, finance, mining, etc.), about 75 major industry groups (e.g., banking, health care, education, etc.), and over 400 industries (e.g., savings banks, hospitals, colleges, etc.). And the special attributes and characteristics of each industry can be identified and reflected in the profession's service approach to that industry.

THE TREND TOWARDS SPECIAL INDUSTRY COMPETENCE

Rather than concentrating on the special needs of the many types of industries that comprise its market, the profession in the past moved somewhat in an opposite direction. As stated in Chapter 7, Auditing's Changing Marketplace, it endeavored to standardize auditing procedures so that they would apply to virtually any company in any industry. These procedures centered around the balance sheet accounts, which, except for variations in nomenclature or terminology, do not vary much among industries. That is to say, cash is cash, receivables are receivables, etc,, no matter in which industry they are found or by whatever names they are called. Under this "universal" approach to auditing, it was at least theoretically possible for an auditor to conduct a financial audit of a strange company in an unfamiliar industry with but a minimum of knowledge about either. The differing characteristics of the various industries were all but lost in the profession's heavy emphasis on verification techniques rather than on the nature of the industry environment in which they were to be applied. Even such authoritative works as the 8th Edition of *Montgomery's Auditing* contained but few references to specific industries. And practice sets used for audit training were invariably built around hypothetical manufacturing companies.

Although there had always been a sprinkling of industry specialists among accountants and accounting firms— "bank men," "brokerage men," and "retail specialists," it was only a decade or so ago that the profession began to emphasize industry characteristics in designing its services and marketing them. No doubt the rash of suits brought against accountants and their firms during the 1960s for failure to discover or properly report vital information concerning companies they audited helped spur this change of emphasis. For it had become increasingly apparent that auditing procedures cannot be so "standardized" as to apply safely to all companies in all industries, and that there are vastly differing industry characteristics that the auditor must know about and take into account in conducting his work, if for no other reason then his own self–protection. One singularly obscure example involved the automobile financing industry's practice of renegotiating "slow loans." Apparently these are sometimes evidenced by new contracts that bear the renegotiation date rather than the original loan date. Accordingly, the auditor could easily over–value the related receivables if he were not aware of this particular industry practice.

In criticizing the auditors for their faulty handling of the audit of *National Student Marketing Corporation*, the SEC observed in Accounting Release 173 in 1975, "the auditors were not sufficiently familiar with the business context to assess the representations of management. . . . Auditors should either possess or avail themselves of sufficient industry knowledge to judge the substance of the situation."

The AICPA Statement on Auditing Standards No. 4, December 1974, suggests the designation of industry specialists as part of auditing quality control mechanisms.

Industry Savvy Helpful in Marketing Accounting Services

Aside from the technical aspects of their work, accountants are now stressing their industry knowledge and competence in marketing their services and expanding their practices. Every businessman considers his operation and industry unique—different from all others. He regards knowledge of his industry as vital, and his confidence in an accountant is influenced by the presence or absence of this knowledgeability. Indeed, familiarity with a business's nature and its jargon is expected of an accountant upon his first appearance on the premises. He is expected to know what's going on in the industry.

All of this is reflected in increased industry emphasis within at least the major accounting firms, and in the relatively recent setting up of special industry committees by the American Institute of CPAs. The Institute has issued some 16 industry audit guides at the time of this writing. And an increasing number of professional publications and articles are centering around specific industries.

THE DIVERSITY OF INDUSTRY CHARACTERISTICS

Industry characteristics are distinctive and diverse. The accountant working with a regulated public utility company, for example, will find a uniform classification of accounts, as well as special accounting principles, reporting practices, and teminology. He will also find that the income tax law grants special deductions or credits to utilities that are not available to other industries. And he will become aware of conflicting requirements of state and federal regulatory agencies that he must understand if he is to be effective on the job.

In financial companies he will find something quite different. Banks' balance sheets, for example, have traditionally been called statements of condition. Banks have no physical inventories. Their plant investment is *relatively* minimal. Their processes are essentially judgmental and clerical, as opposed, for example, to the product assembly line of the manufacturer. Banks have not always seen eye–to–eye with accountants, particularly on such questions as the treatment of loan losses or income from securities transactions. An accountant working in this industry needs to know not only the Federal Reserve Board's requirements concerning reserves, but also the Financial Accounting Standards Board's latest thoughts on bank reporting.

Insurance companies have regulatory problems, too. In addition, they have been undergoing dramatic changes in economics and markets. The casualty companies have been hard hit by losses, particularly judgments in automobile cases. The life companies are becoming increasingly competitive with government insurance programs, such as Medicare, and are themselves striving for position in still another industry through the sale of variable annuities and mutual funds. Insurance companies are moving steadily toward the greater use of independent accountants, not only to meet SEC requirements for their mutual funds, but also to certify their own financial statements which, by the way, are as different from those of a manufacturer as they could possibly be.

Insurance accounting is designed more to protect the policyholder than to inform the stockholder, and the accountant must be aware of the differences between insurance accounting practices and generally accepted accounting principles.

Hospitals and universities have traditionally used fund accounting, although the more progressive among them are adopting more conventional accounting techniques for financial reporting purposes. Hospitals nowadays are deluged with new and more exacting types of paper work as a result of Medicare. And they are being pushed by the Social Security Administration and the Blue Cross to organize their operations better and keep their costs down.

Universities have their own particular brand of financial woes, which are the result, primarily, of overambitious expansion programs coupled with constantly increasing faculty costs. The plight of independent colleges and universities is particularly acute. While a more businesslike approach to operations and finance might save those that are left, a number of marginal schools have already closed their doors or have amalgamated with stronger ones.

Religious institutions have their financial and accounting problems, too, primarily because of their involvement with hospitals and other institutions, particularly parochial school systems. The Catholic Church's biggest single expense, lay faculty salaries, has literally exploded over the years, creating almost unmanageable deficits. The Church is increasingly engaging independent accountants to establish financial reporting systems as well as management controls. Bishop Fulton Sheen was reported by the *Wall Street Journal* some years ago to have engaged independent accountants in the Rochester diocese. He was quoted as saying that the Lord undoubtedly erred when he permitted priests to handle money!

The accountant working with an industrial company will find that it, too, has distinctive characteristics. Not all manufacturers are alike, to start with, and the extractive companies are distinctly different creatures. Their exploration and development activities and depletion charges have spawned a separate and immense encyclopedia of accounting and tax principles.

These are but a few of the differing characteristics of various industries. There are many others. And while the accountant is essentially a generalist and his skills are basic, it is becoming increasingly apparent that a knowledge of industry characteristics is necessary if he is to turn in a competent professional performance and effectively market his services.

Types of Knowledge Needed

The special industry knowledge required by the accountant falls into two broad classes: information of a technical nature—that is, information that is vital to the conduct of the technical practice; and non–technical information—that is, knowledge of general industry developments and intelligence.

Technical information would include a typical chart of accounts or an accounting plan; any unique accounting principles, reporting practices, or terminology; applicable regulatory requirements; and any special income tax treatments in the form of special deductions, credits, or methods of computation. Technical information would also include any prevailing business practices and current economic, regulatory, or technological developments in the industry that may have audit or tax implications—as, for example, in the evaluation of receivables, inventories, reserves, or even obsolescence of plant.

Non–technical information includes general industry intelligence and developments that have no particular technical implications. Nevertheless, knowledge of these is expected of the professional accountant dealing with the industry. This knowledge is usually acquired as a natural by-product of immersion in practice in that industry, by attendance at industry association meetings, or by other contacts with industry people or literature. The accountant must also keep abreast of competition or merger trends within the industry with which he is working, as well as keep track of imminent legislation affecting the industry—the sort of thing that would pervade the "shop talk" at an industry get-together.

ORGANIZING THE PRACTICE BY INDUSTRY

As said earlier, there has always been a sprinkling of industry specialists among accountants and accounting firms, but generally these were limited to industries that were considered the most unique or the most distinctive from an accounting viewpoint—banks, brokerages, savings and loans, insurance companies, hospitals, department stores, and utilities.

The increasing recognition of the importance of an industry approach to accounting practice naturally provokes questions as to how far industry specialization should go and to what extent it should be formalized in a firm's organization.

An individual practitioner or small firm might simply select one or two industries, learn all about them, and concentrate on developing a specialized practice in those industries. On the other hand, a large firm with thousands of clients in many industries theoretically could segregate its practice into a hundred different industry departments, each of which could concentrate solely on serving clients within the particular industry. But only theoretically. For among other things, the firm's operating efficiency and flexibility and the breadth of its perspective would suffer from such extreme compartmentalization. So, probably, would staff morale, since one of the main attractions of public accounting is the variety of industries and businesses to which one is exposed.

Actually, professional specialization is a natural response to expansion in the size, scope, or complexity of a discipline or the subject of its application. Specialization of various types has been evolving continuously in the accounting profession and its various firms since the beginning. Commencing with division and concentration, this process invariably progresses into de facto specialization, and then through various stages of recognition, formalization, and organization. Tax practice is an example. It now includes a series of specialists in many sub–areas, such as reorganizations, estate planning, state taxes, and others.

The degree of industry specialization has varied widely among accounting firms, depending on their size, the capabilities of their personnel, and the nature and demands of their practices. Every firm, for example, invariably takes industry experience into account to some extent and at some level in making its staff and partner assignments. And this is particularly evident when a *new* client is involved.

It seems to follow that accounting firms should recognize, encourage, and accelerate this otherwise natural process by providing a distinct but flexible framework in which it can develop to its furthest extent. The framework need not, indeed should not, be overly rigid, lest it constrict by over-structuring or over–organization.

It might begin with the formation of informal or ad hoc groups of professionals, both partners and staff, who have had extensive experience in particular industries. These would include tax specialists and management consultants, as well as auditors. These groups would stay abreast of developments in the industry; advise in connection with technical accounting matters in the industry; assist in the development of firm training courses, seminars, and conferences in the industry; write books and articles and participate in industry meetings and seminars; attend meetings of industry and trade associations; and generally concern themselves with the conduct of the practice in their industry. This would involve having meetings or other communications between members of the industry groups, assisting in the preparation of proposals to prospective clients in the industry, and monitoring the economics and logistics of the firm's practice in the industry.

As to what constitutes an "industry" for purposes of organizing the specialists would involve factors such as the size of the practice and its make–up by industry, as well as the number of personnel having industry experience. In any event, industries selected for such attention should be identified by reference to the Standard Industrial Classification code numbers, for the code provides a sound framework for future expansion.

The industry groups should report to a firm–wide director or partner in charge of industry competence or specialization. Whether he is to be considered part of the firm's practice function or its marketing function depends on the firm's organizational philosophy, for industry specialization is still somewhat of a hybrid.

Central Industry Library or Files

Finally, a central industry reference library is probably desirable to accumulate industry by industry information from within the firm as well as from appropriate outside sources, and assemble it for use in the conduct of the practice and in obtaining new clients.

CHAPTER 12

The Publics

As pointed out in Chapter 7, the accounting profession's traditional "publics" are now expanding to include the some 25 million shareholders in American industry who ultimately may participate more directly in the selection of their companys' auditors—as well as the vast amorphous public at large, whose approval of the profession is required if it is to continue its present important role. Dealing with these broad publics will require a greater understanding and more aggressive use of the media than heretofore. The profession will simply have to become more sophisticated in mass communications.

There are, however, a number of specific publics that should be acknowledged by an accountant and his firm, not only because of their value in producing new work, but because of their importance in other areas. Educators, for example, can be an important source of new, highly qualified staff. Their opinions concerning the various firms can often influence the graduate's decision concerning which firm he would like to be with.

Some of the publics have been mentioned previously—client officers and directors, for example, as well as college alumni, church, club, and civic associations. But there are others, internal and external. In the interest of completeness, all of accountancy's significant publics are listed here, including those that are mentioned elsewhere in this work.

It will be noted that members of the firm family itself are included in the listing as "internal" publics. Since they are the principal transmitters of the firm's message to those outside the firm, they must be kept informed of developments and constantly "sold," themselves. Yet they are sometimes

overlooked when communications programs are being designed. Partners, particularly of large firms, are often heard
to complain that they are the last to hear of developments
within their own firms.

THE INTERNAL PUBLICS—THE FIRM FAMILY

Partners, Professional Staff, and Administrative Employees

Everyone connected with a firm is a potential salesman and,
if appropriately indoctrinated concerning the firm and its
activities, can at least further its image, if not actually produce new work. Partners and professional staff are, of
course, in everyday contact with the marketplace. But many
administrative employees are, too—particularly secretaries,
receptionists, and telephone operators. They are in constant
contact with the firm's friends and clients and therefore need
to be kept informed of what's going on and encouraged to do
some selling themselves—principally by being pleasant, alert,
and helpful to everyone with whom they come into contact
either personally or by phone.

A pleasant manner can attract—an unpleasant one re-
pel. One chief telephone operator of long standing in her
firm developed an unfortunate snarl in her voice and became
increasingly impatient with callers in her later years. She
made them feel like intruders. She alienated both existing
and potential clients alike—and probably cost the firm hundreds of thousands of dollars in lost work. Why wasn't she
fired? Because everyone was afraid of her, including the
partner in charge—which is reminiscent of that old chestnut
about the company president who called a meeting of the
vice presidents and asked, "Is there anyone here who has not
dated that new red–headed telephone operator?" When one
junior man raised his hand and said, "I haven't," the president barked "Well then you can fire her!"

Spouses

Wives, or, in appropriate cases, husbands, of partners and professional staff are among the important publics of the firm. One of the traditional drawbacks of public accounting practice is the long hours and extensive out–of–town work. This creates a hardship for the accountant's wife and family and is an important factor in decisions to transfer from public accounting to industry.

While a firm can never completely assuage a wife's unhappiness over her husband's frequent absences and the disruptions to their normal family life, it can acknowledge the problem by bringing wives into more frequent contact with the husband's business world and his associates through dinner dances and other social gatherings, or by encouraging (and paying for) their attendance at professional society or even firm meetings.

Sometimes, a delicate situation can develop, as wives become accustomed to attending these affairs, and situations arise that require a change in policy. The partner in charge of one firm's partners' meeting, which was held annually at a particularly sumptuous resort hotel and traditionally included wives, was at a loss on how to notify the wives that they were *not* to be invited that year. He explained to the firm's public relations counselor that there were several reasons for the change in practice. A greater proportion of the meeting time was to be devoted to business—breakfast meetings, luncheon meetings, and even late night sessions were to be added, and there simply would not be enough time for social occasions. "Besides," the partner added "the firm has gotten so big, the hotel can no longer accomodate the wives."

"What was that again, George?" the PR man asked. "Did you say there's no room for the wives?" "Never mind all those other reasons," he added, "just tell them there isn't any room."

When thoroughly interested in their husband's work and kept informed of developments in his firm, wives can often spot a new client opportunity faster than their husbands.

Retired Partners and Firm Alumni

Retired partners can be invaluable to their old firms if their interest can be maintained—something that is sometimes lost sight of by their younger successors, who frequently disdain all that went before. The retired partner's principal contribution does not usually arise from his technical knowledge as much as from his broad knowledge and position in the important social and cultural community. Given some encouragement, he can often help the younger partners become established in important new client marketplaces in the community. He and his wife can open doors that would ordinarily remain closed to the younger people for years to come.

Maintaining contact with retired partners—providing them with desk space and part–time stenographic help, keeping them on the firm's mailing list, and including them in important social functions of the firm, will keep them pulling for the firm. Otherwise, they will likely sign off and move to Florida.

Alumni of the firm, former partners or staff who left to take positions in industry, government, or not–for–profit organizations, have a natural loyalty to their old firm and, if recognized and encouraged, will recommend it at every opportunity. Many firms add alumni members to their mailing list immediately upon their departure and otherwise remain in touch with them through annual golf outings or other social or recreational events.

THE EXTERNAL PUBLICS

Individual Income Tax Clients–Proprietorships

The individual income tax client and, indeed, the small proprietorship live in fear of income tax audits and the Internal

Revenue Service. Incidentally, many accountants do too—when their own returns are involved. The individual is reluctant to attempt to prepare his own tax return because of the possibility that he may commit a grievous error, bringing down the awesome power of this branch of government upon his head. So he turns to the accountant to prepare his return, not only because it is a difficult and distasteful task for most laymen, but because a CPA's name on the return is thought to lend respectability and stature, and it serves to discourage the over–zealous tax examiner from throwing the book at the hapless taxpayer. Besides, the CPA is experienced in dealing with tax examiners and can be expected to represent his client well—often without the taxpayer being present. A blessing!

None but the most calloused accountant will fail to recognize how much he is needed and appreciated by his individual income tax and proprietorship clients. The only comment that is appropriate here is that individuals tend to express their relief at having their income tax problems lifted off their shoulders by boasting high and wide about how great their accountants are. They are usually the least expensive and most vociferous form of professional advertising.

Client Management, Directors, and Stockholders

Management today is as much a profession as medicine, law, or accountancy—due principally to the increase in the number of business administration programs at both the undergraduate and graduate levels, as well as in the continuing education programs sponsored by the American Management Association and other professional organizations. A monumental body of classified knowledge has developed over the last 40 years on the art and science of managing people and resources. And new procedures, methods, and techniques are promptly cataloged and disseminated throughout the entire management community through an efficient network of management books and magazines.

The professional manager is an important figure in an industrial society—and the American manager is particularly important, because of the immense power he wields in the publicly owned company. For all practical purposes, a professional manager, as a company's chief executive officer, is often in de facto control despite the legal prerogatives of the board of directors or stockholders. He reports to the board of directors, who are in turn elected by the stockholders. But more often than not he selects the candidates—and they support and back him in most of his recommendations. The board can, and sometimes does, overrule management, but in the past this was more the exception than the rule.

The officers of publicly held companies want no public disagreements or disputes with the auditors. They want the auditors' approval. They want a "clean" (unqualified) opinion on the company's financial statements. And they do not want to have to backtrack on earnings announcements or estimates. They do not want to be unpleasantly surprised by large adjustments to their earnings at year's end. They also want to be kept informed of what's happening in the business arena.

Most accounting firms stay in touch with management during the year to discuss and settle differences and doubts in connection with accounting and financial reporting problems as they arise—particularly when quarterly earnings are being announced. Auditors are becoming increasingly associated with interim earnings figures as a result of the new SEC requirement contained in Accounting Release 177.

Management and Auditor Selection. Management has always had a strong voice in the selection of auditors. Whenever changes have occurred, it has almost always been management who would initiate the change and recommend the new auditors for approval by the stockholders. And the stockholders invariably have rubber stamped management's recommendation.

This is changing. Audit committees composed of outside members of boards of directors are taking over this function; where accountants formerly dealt principally with management in connection with the terms of an engagement, they will increasingly deal with audit committees in the future. The committees establish a close relationship with the company's auditors and act as their principal point of contact; they elicit any complaints or problems the auditors may have in dealing with management and vice versa; they deal with the auditors on the scope of the engagement and any special assignments; and they negotiate the fee. Finally, they recommend the auditors or any changes in auditing firms to the full board, which brings these recommendations to the shareholders at the annual meeting. (See The Metcalf Committee's Recommendations in Chapter 9, The U. S. Profession.)

It is possible that the stockholders will one day participate more directly in the selection of auditors, particularly when tensions have developed between the auditors and the board, and the auditors decide to make a strong public bid to hold the engagement.

What a novel proxy fight!

However, at the time of this writing the audit committee of the board of directors is still the focal point for the selection or retention of auditors.

Outside Directors. In recent years directors have become increasingly concerned with the problem of liability and how to protect themselves. Doubts are increasing as to whether boards are conscientiously carrying out their traditional function—whether individual board members, for example, are being sufficiently alert and objective to protect the interests of the stockholders and others who rely on them. This concern has been heightened by a few highly publicized cases of director dereliction. Suits and threats of suit have multiplied. The trend of court decisions has created considerable uneasiness in corporate boardrooms.

Outside directors have felt especially uncomfortable

and vulnerable. Unlike inside directors, they are not intimately familiar with the company and its operations and are not privy to what management is doing. They are not in a position to detect and call a halt to unsavory or illegal activities.

These troubled directors, who often comprise the board's audit committee, are increasingly looking to the company's independent auditors for assurances that management is performing properly and prudently and in the best interests of the stockholders. They are particularly interested in the accountants' appraisal of the company's internal controls and other safeguards against the company's getting off the track.

Alert accountants will furnish the necessary assurances through personal visits with the outside directors and by making certain that they are furnished copies of letters to management concerning internal controls and similar matters.

Other Professionals

Other professionals are second only to existing clients as a source of new clients. Other professionals include other accountants, lawyers, bankers and investment bankers.

Other Accountants. Large firms frequently refer engagements to smaller firms. The work may be of a type that the smaller firm specializes in or is particularly equipped to handle, or the engagement may simply be too small for the large firm's multiple and often costly review procedures. One individual practitioner in Philadelphia developed a special expertise in establishing the amounts of losses from fires and other casualties. He was kept busy simply handling referrals from other accountants.

Conversely, small accounting firms sometimes refer engagements to large firms. The usual occasion is when the client needs a special service that only a large firm can pro-

vide, or when the client is about to go public and the underwriters insist on having a "name" auditing firm. Naturally,
the small accountant will recommend the firm in which he
has the greatest confidence, and this, incidentally, is apt to be
the one that has referred work to him or otherwise man-
ifested a sincere interest.

Whether a firm is large or small, it should recognize
other firms or practitioners as possible sources of new client
referrals and cultivate them accordingly. One way to go
about this is by speaking at professional society meetings or
writing for professional journals on the subject of one's
specialty. SEC experts from a large firm, for example,
might speak or write on such subjects as, "So Your Client is
Going Public," and small firm participants on "Overcoming
Inventory Problems in the Small Business."

Lawyers. Accountants have a great deal in common
with lawyers because of the similarity of much of their work,
and because they work so closely together on client
matters—especially on taxes and SEC filings. Ultimately the
members of the two professions develop a deep respect for
the other's technical knowledge and expertise, and this
naturally leads to a recommendation or referral when the
occasion presents itself.

Accountants usually gain an understanding of the in-
tricacies of new business tax laws earlier than lawyers, because their work requires them to compute tax provisions for
financial statement purposes promptly and to prepare returns. Sharing the results of their initial research and analysis
of a new tax law with lawyers by furnishing them with tax
bulletins or tax letters is usually appreciated. The same is
true of developments in other areas of mutual interest—SEC
accounting matters, financial reporting, and certain industry
matters, for example. Above all, lawyers are interested in
whatever accountants can tell them about the organization
and administration of a professional service firm—time
charges, client ledgers, income statements, operating
budgets, and sources of capital, for example.

One large accounting firm has prepared a formal
monograph for its lawyer friends on the administration of a
law practice. Another furnishes its friends in the legal profession with complimentary copies of an authoritative work
on SEC accounting practice by one of its partners. Both are
thoughtful gestures that surely must pay for themselves
many times over in work referrals.

Bankers. Accountants also have much in common with
bankers. Indeed, the histories of the two professions are so
parallel and they have reacted so similarly to external forces,
that it would seem they must surely be branches of the same
family tree.

Actually, some accounting firms in Switzerland and
Germany were founded by banks to investigate and monitor
companies to which they made commerical loans. The accounting wings ultimately separated from their banking
affiliations, but, as is pointed out in Chapter 7, Auditing's
Changing Marketplace, the early influence has persisted to
this day. European accounting firms still serve as executors
and trustees, as well as registrars and transfer agents, functions customarily performed in the United States by banks.

Also, accountants and bankers are usually classified together in psychological behavior studies. A survey of high
school students, teachers, and Stanford undergraduates in
the late 1960s, for example, rated the propensities of accountants, bankers, lawyers, and scientists for certain specific be-
haviors.

The accountant was seen as most likely to straighten a
picture in a house where he is a visitor. And, after bankers,
most likely to beat his children for disobeying him. Also, the
accountant was seen as least likely to talk back to a police-
man—and as reluctant as a banker to join a protest march.

The respondents in the survey were given a list of de-
scriptive adjectives and asked which words were most characteristic of the different professions. Accountants were seen as
least understanding, least emotional, dullest, least intelligent,
stiffest, and "as unfriendly as a banker."

It is surprising that this survey found both professions dull, unimaginative, and stuffy as late as the 1960s. One would have thought that they had both reformed since the 1930s, when accountants were seen as "green-eye-shade people without bowels or the milk of human kindness"—and bankers were painted variously as "stuffed shirts and steely-eyed monsters in whose veins ran expensive Kentucky bourbon turned to ice water, and whose heads moved only horizontally."

Jackson Martindell, former chairman of the American Institute of Management, noted that bank buildings in the 1930s and most of the 1940s apparently were designed to convey an impression of solidity, integrity, and conservatism. He thought they looked like mausoleums. But had he visited a few accountants' offices at that time, he would have observed a similarly barren decor. Window draperies, for example, were invariably omitted as being too showy. Explained one grizzled veteran, "Our clients would never stand for such fancy stuff."

David Rockefeller charged that banks in those earlier days did not respond as alertly as they might have to the increasingly complex demands of the times. Accountancy, too, had a record of stark conservatism and reluctance to make innovations.

But both banks and accounting firms responded to the changing needs of the postwar period in a remarkably similar manner. Banks added a wide variety of lending and financing services. Accountants added a wide variety of management services. Banks expanded geographically through branch banking, chain banking, and bank holding companies. Accountants acquired many new locations in additional cities. American banks moved overseas. So did American accounting firms. Banks began to classify their markets by reference to industries and to build specialized industry knowledge in their personnel. So did accountants.

Banks have moved heavily into advertising and promotion, using all types of modes and media. They have replaced their once bland institutional advertising with multicolored promotions built around central themes or slogans. Accounting, too, is embracing modern marketing and communications techniques—although more slowly.

With all these affinities suggesting a near blood-brother relationship, one would think that bankers would be an excellent source of client referrals for accountants. Actually, they are—particularly if the accountant maintains a sizable balance in the bank. Bankers tend to be somewhat influenced by money, which is not surprising considering the nature of their business.

Actually, bankers are both primary and third-party users of accountants' services. They engage accountants to examine their own financial statements, and to perform so called "directors' examinations" as well. And they are buyers of tax services and management services. But they also depend on accountants' reports in evaluating the credit worthiness of applicants for business loans. The accountant in such cases acts as somewhat of an intermediary. He aids the banker by supplying credible financial information concerning his client, and he aids the client by helping him obtain necessary financing.

Finally, banks are a source of working capital for accounting firms, particularly during the middle half of the year, when client receivables are at their highest level.

Bankers truly merit accountants' attention and respect—and possibly even their affection.

Investment Bankers. Accountants work closely with investment bankers, principally in connection with SEC filings. As pointed out in Chapter 8, The Special Services, they advise on questions relating to the financial information required by the SEC. They issue "comfort letters" to the underwriters indicating that their review of unaudited interim financial statements revealed nothing reflecting on the fairness of the overall presentation; and they review indentures relating to proposed new issues of securities, as well as underwriting agreements, and applications for listing on securities exchanges.

There is little need for accountants to seek proximity to investment bankers or underwriters. They are constantly working with them on client matters. They simply need to perform well—for investment bankers are a primary referral source and will recommend those accountants in whom they have confidence.

College and University Accounting Faculties

Everything else being equal, the firms that consistently obtain the top ranking graduates will just as consistently outstrip others in quality and growth. The competition for the top accounting graduates is intense. The battle of the recruiting brochures, described in Chapter 15, The Communications Function—is one manifestation of this competitiveness. The most desirable candidates are wooed by practically all firms, and they receive offers from most. But their decisions as to which to accept are frequently influenced by faculty advisors or placement officers who endeavor to keep abreast of developments in the profession and the firms in order to provide appropriate guidance.

Under the circumstances, faculty members and placement officers are very important to accounting firms, and most firms that recruit regularly on college campuses endeavor to visit with these people and cultivate them. In most cases the recruiter contacts them during his annual visit to the campus.

Some firms, however, make a special point of furnishing college accounting departments and faculties with the firm's technical publications and pronouncements, particularly the more provocative ones. And they offer their top technical people for appearances before college classes and seminars where they can stimulate student and faculty thought—and imagination. Prominent accountants also work with the American Accounting Association, the national organization of accounting academicians, and appear on their technical programs.

Also, a number of firms have established annual grant and gift programs for schools of accountancy—and some have endowed chairs in accounting usually in the name of a revered deceased partner. Still others engage prominent professors or instructors to assist in firm research programs during the summer.

All of these activities, of course, are an acknowledgment of the profession's responsibilities to its academic origins, as well as to the main source of its continuing life blood—good people.

Alumni Associations. There is something to be gained from active participation in one's college alumni association. In the beginning, the graduate is looked to principally for the payment of annual dues. But, as he or she advances in the business or professional world, opportunities open up for committee chairmanships or even high office in the alumni association. Since a reasonable percentage of graduates of most schools ultimately achieve some position and affluence, an accountant's alumni association activities offer an opportunity to stay in touch.

Government Officials

Accountants practice before many federal, state, and local government departments and commissions in the course of serving their clients. These include the SEC and the Internal Revenue Service. They also include the Federal Power Commission, the Interstate Commerce Commission, the Federal Communications Commission, as well as various state utility commissions and state and local tax authorities—just to name a few.

The accountant will encounter a great many less–than–competent individuals while practicing before these departments. Some are inept, others lazy, and still others are simply too resentful to be of service. These people are to be diplomatically but firmly avoided.

On the other hand, government work attracts many highly motivated and fair–minded people who wish to be of genuine service and will go out of their way to expedite a ruling or break a bureaucratic log jam. A deep mutual respect can develop between the responsible government people and the professionals who practice before their departments. They are worth cultivating, for they can be of genuine service—sometimes in the most unexpected way.

Revenue Agent Jones (not his real name) proposed to disallow a deduction of several hundred thousand dollars claimed by an electric utility company in its income tax return. The company asked the author to confer with Jones in the IRS office. They were joined by a Mr. Smith (also not his real name), who was the revenue agent in charge. The conference began at 11 A.M.

The author cited a number of authorities and precedents in support of the company's position that the expenditure was deductible in the year it was claimed—that it was not a capital expenditure that would ordinarily be amortized or depreciated over future years. But Jones refused to concede. The author presented additional authorities and arguments in support of the deduction. Jones still refused to concede. Around noon time Mr. Smith, who had remained quiet for the entire time, got up and left, and returned an hour later. (It later developed that he had simply gone out to lunch.)

At about 1:30, the author said to Jones, "I feel as though I've been talking to a stone wall. I've given you at least twenty reasons why this item is deductible, and you haven't cited even one authority to support its disallowance."

"I've shot my bolt," the author continued, "but before I leave I would be interested to know what your boss, Mr. Smith, thinks about this item."

The agent turned to Smith and asked, "Oh yes, Mr. Smith, what do you think about it?"

"It's obviously deductible," Smith replied. "That became apparent in the first two minutes."

The author gathered his papers together and left with

the growing realization that he had been temporarily drafted and had unwittingly served in the Internal Revenue Service's training corps.

There are many Joneses in the government. But there are also enough Smiths to keep the government moving—and they should be treated with great deference.

Executive Directors of Trade and Industry Associations

Most business, trade, and industry associations, are administered by professional secretaries or executive directors. They report to the president or chairman, who is appointed or elected by the board of directors, who in turn are a self-renewing body. The ultimate power in these organizations often resides in the professional administrators, since they are engaged full time and are permanent where the others are not. The professional arranges annual meetings and meetings of the board, sets agendas, supervises staff research, and otherwise carries on the work of the association. Invariably he or she becomes publicly identified with the organization as its principal spokesman.

Executive directors are an important public. An accountant who seeks to participate actively in an association's activities or to appear on its programs should make himself known to the professional who runs it—for he has the ultimate power over committee appointments and programs.

PART IV

A FIRMWIDE
MARKETING FUNCTION

THE MARKETING—PUBLIC RELATIONS—
COMMUNICATIONS FUNCTION

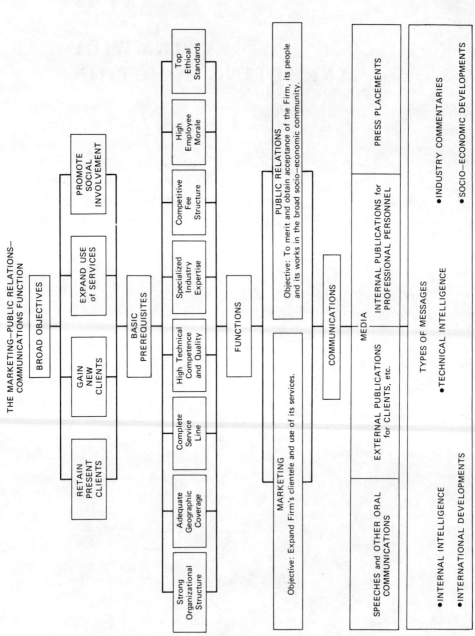

BROAD OBJECTIVES

| RETAIN PRESENT CLIENTS | GAIN NEW CLIENTS | EXPAND USE of SERVICES | PROMOTE SOCIAL INVOLVEMENT |

BASIC PREREQUISITES

| Strong Organizational Structure | Adequate Geographic Coverage | Complete Service Line | High Technical Competence and Quality | Specialized Industry Expertise | Competitive Fee Structure | High Employee Morale | Top Ethical Standards |

FUNCTIONS

MARKETING
Objective: Expand Firm's clientele and use of its services.

PUBLIC RELATIONS
Objective: To merit and obtain acceptance of the Firm, its people and its works in the broad socio—economic community.

COMMUNICATIONS

MEDIA

| SPEECHES and OTHER ORAL COMMUNICATIONS | EXTERNAL PUBLICATIONS for CLIENTS, etc. | INTERNAL PUBLICATIONS for PROFESSIONAL PERSONNEL | PRESS PLACEMENTS |

TYPES OF MESSAGES

- INTERNAL INTELLIGENCE
- INTERNATIONAL DEVELOPMENTS
- TECHNICAL INTELLIGENCE
- INDUSTRY COMMENTARIES
- SOCIO—ECONOMIC DEVELOPMENTS

Figure 2   Marketing, Public Relations, Communications Function

CHAPTER 13

Embracing The Marketing Concept

Marketing is usually thought of in terms of product design, packaging, and display; selling, advertising, and promotion; or indeed even warehousing and distribution. Actually, all are valid aspects of marketing. But the total concept is considerably bigger than the sum of these.

Marketing is an aura that pervades an organization and everyone in it. It is a will to expand and grow and *to be of service*. Indeed, marketing ranks with finance and production as one of the topmost functions of a business, and in some respects it is the most important of all. For it provides the organizational spark that ignites the principal systems and functions, and it monitors their progress. It originates the business plan as to what shall be produced, where and how it will be sold, and within limits, at what price. It is the principal interface between an organization and its markets. More than any other function, it seeks to expand volume and profits by ascertaining the needs and demands of customers or clients, and satisfying them.

THE CHANGING PROFESSIONAL ATTITUDES

When asked why he had selected a particular firm as his company's auditors over several other firms he had interviewed, the company president replied, "because they exhibited a genuine interest in our needs." Pointing to several of the firm's publications on his desk, he added, "I'm not particularly interested in those booklets and probably won't read them." "But," he added, "the fact that the firm took the trouble to produce these and hand them to me tells me that they are interested in us and want to serve us."

"Moreover," he went on, "the firm's partners conveyed the same interest with their lean–forward attitude during our meeting." "In contrast," he continued, "the representatives of the other firms seemed standoffish and aloof—in fact, they acted as though they were doing us a favor in responding to our inquiry."

This incident occurred during the 1950s. In retrospect, it probably marked the beginning of a change in the accounting profession's attitude toward the use of marketing concepts in building a practice. Of course, the first firms to adopt traditional marketing techniques were looked upon as more than just avant–garde by their professional peers—they were considered upstarts, and even unprofessional.

Most members of the profession were still concentrating on technical matters, not growth, and they were reluctant to initiate activities that might be construed as an overt effort to gain new clients.

The profession had been conservative from the beginning. Its members relied principally on technical books, papers, and talks to enhance their professional reputation, and on recommendations by existing clients and bankers for new clients. The profession frowned upon any actions or programs that were designed to attract new clients directly—and the proselytizing of a fellow professional's client or any other encroachment on his practice was a matter for possible censure.

When approached by another accountant's client who wants to change auditors, it has long been customary for a professional to notify the other accountant before accepting the engagement. One reason for this is to ascertain from the previous auditor whether there is any reason for *not* accepting the engagement—for example, no accountant wants to inherit a client that has a propensity for fraud. Another reason is simple professional courtesy.

The notification requirement has not always been followed, of course—and no doubt it is often followed reluctantly. But the fact that the custom has existed suggests the relatively restrained nature of the professional environment. Accountants have long held in check their more rapacious competitive instincts.

Actually, the CPA degree in itself was enough to attract new clients in the days before World War II. While the public was somewhat vague about the CPA's work, many had heard of his extensive training qualifications and the rigorous examination he had to pass. And the aura of mystery and aloofness in which the profession cloaked itself no doubt added to the respect and awe with which the CPA was regarded.

One veteran partner of a major firm summed up the prevailing atmosphere when he said, "Our firm doesn't have to go after new clients. Because of our great reputation, prospects walk in the door in droves, and we simply decide whether or not we will take them."

Diverging from the Needs of the Marketplace

As suggested in Chapter 7, Auditing's Changing Marketplace, the profession probably had begun to diverge from the needs of its marketplace by the 1940s. Where the adoption of the two–way communications techniques that are ordinarily part of the marketing process might have alerted the profession to changing needs and preferences of its clients, it continued to remain aloof, although in this respect it was probably no different than the legal and medical professions.

In most industries, marketing people work with technicians in designing and packaging the product. Consumer needs and preferences thus are acknowledged, if not satisfied. This has not been so in the professions. There the technicians have traditionally designed the product. They rarely consult the user. They usually decide what is best for him. They develop the procedures and techniques—and that's what the consumer gets. (Someone once quipped that a profession is a conspiracy against the laity!)

Accountancy is no exception. Its principal product, auditing, was designed and developed by technicians with one overriding purpose: to enable the auditor to express his opinion on the fairness of presentation of a company's financial condition and the results of its operations—and no more. Of course, this was a pretty important purpose—in the light of the immense credibility independent auditors have added to financial statements on which investors and lenders rely. Modern auditing techniques and procedures were designed to achieve that purpose efficiently and economically.

But *only* that purpose.

They were not designed or intended to uncover defalcations or other irregularities, such as illegal political contributions or bribes to foreign officials. Nor were they designed to familiarize the auditor sufficiently with the company's operations or its industry problems to make intelligent suggestions to management concerning productivity or profitability.

At one time, auditing did these things—it produced these by-products. But that was when businesses were considerably smaller, and auditors were able to verify most transactions. But as businesses grew in size and complexity, auditing was streamlined in the interests of economy. Greater stress was placed on the effectiveness of internal controls, including those now implicit in computer systems. And the by–products suffered.

Yet many of accountancy's ultimate consumers, particularly the smaller investors, still believe that regular examinations by independent auditors will reveal irregularities, and that the auditors are keeping management on the track by monitoring the company's operations. And they refuse to be dissuaded from relying on auditors for these purposes.

Moreover, many *within* the profession believe that audit procedures and techniques should be extended to operations sufficiently to enable auditors to furnish intelligent suggestions to management concerning productivity and profitability—if for no other reason than that this is expected of CPAs by their publics.

Also, many within the profession endorse a specialized

industry approach to accounting practice, because it equips the auditor to deal more knowledgeably with client problems. Of course, both productivity suggestions to management and specialized industry competence have a marketing appeal that far exceeds that of historical auditing, which, notwithstanding its great contribution to credibility and capital markets, is staid indeed.

Actually, the need to furnish constructive operating suggestions to management had been regularly voiced by members of the profession for over a half–century. It was urged in the *Journal of Accountancy* as early as 1914. And the need for specialized industry competence was cited repeatedly in professional journals over the years.

But, as also pointed out in Chapter 7, most firms had moved in the opposite direction in the intervening years. The concept of auditing became perceptively narrower, as the two–paragraph, short–form auditor's report gradually superceded the long–form reports that had traditionally included detailed comments on the client's operations, as well as its financial condition. Post–audit comments to management then became largely limited to financial control matters—as contrasted with operations.

Ironically, most large firms meanwhile had acquired an independent management consulting competence that included the very techniques needed for infusing productivity improvement aspects into financial audits. But they did not get around to fully deploying them.

Even after it had become apparent in the 1950s that those few firms that had embraced the marketing concept were growing very rapidly, most firms were slow to adopt the marketing approach. A conservative professional attitude continued to prevail. There was a general reluctance, for example, to issue directories showing a firm's office locations and personnel; or booklets describing its services or listing its clients, or, indeed mentioning anything concerning the firm's revenues, profits, or numbers of personnel.

That the firm's clients might find such information interesting and even helpful was never denied. But neither was it stressed. Rather, the atmosphere was pervaded by fears that such published documents would fall into the "wrong hands"—that is, into the hands of non–clients—and that they would be construed as prima facie evidence of an intent by the issuing firm to attract those non–clients. Since some firms were beginning to issue newsletters and other information pieces, professional ethics committees placed the responsibility on the issuing firms for controlling the distribution and, by inference, the final destination of their publications. Technical books written by firm members or personnel and published commercially were of course acceptable, and always had been.

Sometime during the 1960s, the dam burst, and practically every firm began to utilize marketing techniques to a lesser or greater degree, spurred no doubt by the now obvious success of the few firms that had embraced the marketing concept 10 years earlier.

But not until the merger wave had spent itself.

The Merger Wave

During the 1960s, when the attitude concerning growth efforts was still ambivalent, many firms turned to mergers with other accounting firms as a principal source of growth. Indeed, a large part of the phenomenal expansion of the big U.S. accounting firms during the 1960s was attributable to mergers with other accounting firms. The few large firms absorbed hundreds of small and medium–sized firms during that era. The principal objectives, of course, were volume and coverage. Overhead costs were increasing rapidly, as new services were added and new administrative programs installed—and greater volume was needed to absorb these. And geographic dispersion of clients spurred a need for substantial offices in many cities.

In most firms, marketing talents were still scarce, and

opening new offices and attracting new clients by conventional marketing methods seemed exasperatingly slow and expensive.

Mergers, on the other hand, offered a seemingly simple means of expanding locations and building volume. Most major firms devoted extensive time and effort to seeking merger candidates and negotiating with them. Their principal inducement was their formidable recruiting and training apparatus and retirement benefits plans—none of which could be afforded by the smaller firms.

Some mergers worked out very well indeed. But a great many turned out poorly because of unreconcilable differences in personalities and practice standards.

In several cases, the principal "gift" the merged firms brought to the marriage was an incipient lawsuit. A small firm acquired by one of the Big 12 firms in 1972, for example, apparently was already seriously involved in the infamous *Equity Funding* fraud. And the acquiring firm became an unwitting party to the legal actions that ensued.

Another firm found itself operating a wholesale building supply house in receivership to atone for damages wrought by a merged partner who had attested to questionable inventory figures both before and after the merger.

But by and large, most merger problems arose simply from attempting to assimilate large numbers of new people and clients. The digestion process was slow and painful. Indeed, the winners of the many–offices accounting race, like the winners of a pie–eating contest, probably turned out not to be winners at all.

Possibly more serious in the long run was the effect the merger wave probably had on the will to grow by natural means. Since seven– or eight–digit increments in firm revenues could be realized by acquiring an existing practice, it was often reasoned, why should one devote much effort to attempting to acquire a "mere" $5,000 or $10,000 new client? That the future profits from a merged practice were sometimes bargained away to the merged partners to the detriment of the acquiring partners, was apparently lost sight of in the quest for volume.

The merger movement hit its peak around the middle 1960s and receded as firms began to seriously consider a more conventional marketing approach.

By 1975, practically all firms had adopted some types of marketing practices, although few were totally committed to the overall concept. A questionnaire sent to 150 firms in Virginia and responded to by 73 revealed that there was roughly a 50% commitment to the 19 marketing practices that were enumerated. Ninety percent of the firms reported that they regularly evaluate fee policies and client needs, but only 17% reported having a methodical approach to identifying major potential users of their services and adopting means of reaching them. (See Figure 3.)

A reluctance to directly woo the clients of other firms is still strong in the profession. And the maintenance of a formal list of *non*–clients is still believed to reflect an intent to encroach on the practices of others—particularly if accompanied by the practice of assigning partners or staff to "cultivate" these non–clients.

Actually, wide–awake accountants have always kept their eyes on potential clients in the community and managed to become acquainted with them socially or otherwise, without the maintenance of formal lists or the making of specific assignments. It is the formality of the effort that seems to bother most accountants. Somehow it is considered commercialistic and predatory.

At this point in the history of the accounting profession there is still no need to adopt a professional attitude that borders on direct solicitation of clients of another firm. In fact, the Code of Ethics prohibits the "direct uninvited" solicitation of *any* specific potential client. But unless members of the profession can rid themselves of senseless inhibitions against maintaining information files concerning potential markets for their services which of necessity must include

*Figure 3 Marketing Practices of 73 Virginia CPA Firms
Results of A Study by William R. George Ph.D. and
Richard M. Murray CPA*

Activity	Percentage of Firms Performing
Service Offering	
Periodically reexamine services offered	81
Determine which new services to offer	80
Estimate the size of client base for new services	49
Determine share of market for present services	43
Establish written goals and policies	43
Define specific client groups to be served, e.g., retailers, manufacturers, professionals, etc.	29
Communication	
Develop an overall informational approach, identify major users and select methods for reaching them	17
Develop specific informational approaches, such as brochures, seminars, etc.	27
Develop public relations programs understandable to nonaccountants	26
Location	
Analyze potential locations for new offices	40
Evaluate volume and trends at existing locations to see if a move is indicated	38
Fee Structure	
Evaluate fee policies on a systematic basis	90
Collect information on competitors' fees on a systematic basis	17
Market Research	
Evaluate clients' needs	90
Study why people "buy" their services	37
Study who are key influences in engaging the services offered	46
Train and motivate firm members to feedback information about clients' needs and problems	77
Determine the firm's "image" among clients and the general public	84
Study profit trends by service categories and client categories	59

non–clients, they will find it difficult to accept the other aspects of marketing. And most of these aspects are not only wholesome and appropriate for the profession, they are indispensable tools in today's environment.

Aside from the importance of attracting new clients to replace those that are lost from natural causes, and to provide long–term growth generally, there is the problem of maintaining special service staffs and keeping them busy. Accounting firms employ thousands of people in many locations. An increasing proportion of these people are engaged in special work, such as special accounting assignments and tax and management consulting. Unlike traditional year-end auditing and tax engagements, which recur year after year and which can be counted on in staff planning, special engagements are *not* recurring. Each must be separately contracted for and performed as it occurs. The occurrence cannot be left to chance without risking economic disaster through costly periods of staff idleness. Clients and other prospects must be kept constantly apprised of the nature of these services and their applications, so that work can be developed in an even flow.

A well–planned marketing and communications program helps to achieve this. It seeks out, develops, and maintains the market for accounting and related services at consistent levels and enables intelligent staff planning.

PROVIDING A GROWTH ATMOSPHERE

To be effective, the marketing concept must be embraced fully and wholeheartedly. It must be allowed to pervade the organization. An atmosphere conducive to growth should be provided.

This is a function of leadership.

A growth atmosphere is an intangible. It is a mood or frame of mind. It is marked by a spirit of optimism, enthusiasm, zeal, and fervor in the organization, an all pervasive pride in its product and its leadership, and a confidence that they are the best in their field.

Providing and maintaining such an atmosphere is a vital function of leadership. High human spirit is essential to the successful and thriving organization. And while technical efficiency can be delegated to subordinates, inspiration and encouragement must come from the leaders. They must stand wholeheartedly behind the marketing effort and let this be known throughout their organization.

Leaders differ, of course. They have varying styles and characteristics, which tend to be reflected in their firms, particularly if the leaders are in high command for a sufficient period to conform the firm to their ideas or image. The thrust in a firm's development will usually reflect the dominant characteristics of the leading personalities of a given era—individuals who may or may not be in titular command of the firm, but who nevertheless strongly influence its ultimate nature.

Colonel Montgomery's earlier influence on Lybrand is an example. And there is ample evidence of the influence of William Black and Leonard Spacek, as well as Arthur Foye and Thomas Higgins, on their particular firms—Peat, Marwick, Mitchell; Arthur Andersen; Haskins & Sells; and Arthur Young, respectively. The characteristics, personalities, and styles of these leaders differed. But, the dominant characteristic in each case was reflected in the particular firm's overall posture or character.

While there is a tendency to consider all professional firms alike, they are in fact quite different—each has its own distinctive personality. One firm may be marked by a preponderance of extroverted salesmen, another by industrious technicians, and still others by thoughtful analysts or commanding generalists. And these distinctions tend to persist; they perpetuate themselves. Contrary to the old maxim, it is not opposites that attract in human relationships—but likes. Marriage, for example, invariably couples people of the same physical type. There are exceptions, of course, but the point is that they are precisely that—exceptions.

Firms tend to attract the types of people that most resemble their particular character or image. One experienced recruiter boasted that he could predict which of several accounting firms a particular candidate would join, based primarily on his personality and physical type! Several types that come to mind were "tall, dark, and conservative," "blonde, freckled, and brassy," and "short, compact, and quiet."

Marketing efforts must take cognizance of these distinctions in leaders and firms. What may be appropriate for one firm may not be suitable for another. And sometimes there is a need to modify to accommodate a long–term change in the nature of a firm—or to completely recast the approach if it was misjudged in the first place.

An organization predominated by self–motivated professionals who can sell their services effectively and perform them well would not need a heavily structured marketing program. It would experience phenomenal growth without it. For the basic or "natural" method of achieving professional growth lies in a viable initial person-to-person contact and the effective nurturing of the continuing relationship.

But this is a wishful ideal. Professional accountants are naturally and by training disposed more toward professional practice than selling. If left to their own devices, they probably would elect to immerse themselves in technical and professional matters. They require an inspirational atmosphere to spark or at least condone their selling efforts, and they need a growth–oriented leadership.

An essential of such leadership is the ability to personally contribute to growth and to inspire others in the organization to do the same. The appeal may be to fear, self respect, sense of responsibility, pride of accomplishment, affection, loyalty, or even financial recompense. But, whatever the motivation, the leader must let it be known that he is solidly behind the marketing effort; that he considers growth important; and that individual growth efforts will be rewarded.

ESTABLISHING MARKETING OBJECTIVES AND GOALS

Whether an individual accountant is undertaking to build a practice from scratch or a firm is endeavoring to expand an existing practice, goals should be adopted concerning the type and size of practice that is to be sought and the time frame in which this is to be accomplished. And the manpower and money needed to achieve these goals should be appropriated. Naturally, the objectives should be reasonable and achievable. A small practitioner or firm, for example, undoubtedly should focus on obtaining small or medium–sized clients, while the large firm can more logically go after publicly owned companies.

Or, rough parameters may be adopted for determining at what point to open new offices and where. Ernst & Ernst for years apparently pursued a policy of having small offices in many locations, while Price Waterhouse concentrated on a fewer number of very large offices.

Whether the practice should specialize in particular industries also might be a subject of policy. Many smaller accounting firms have built thriving practices by concentrating on specific industries such as banks, savings and loans, hospitals, or mining or insurance companies. While many of these "industry" firms ultimately succumbed to the merger blandishments of the major firms and were absorbed, others still continue to exist and thrive, as, for example, Harris, Kerr, Forster, which specializes in hotels, restaurants, and clubs.

Many opportunities still exist in industry specialization for both large and small firms. Indeed, it probably offers the *single best approach* to building a practice.

Naturally, any objectives or goals adopted should be

communicated to all departments, divisions, and sections in the organization, not only to gain everyone's support for the marketing program, but so that the growth demands can be reflected in operating budgets. One firm's marketing people once forecasted a substantially increased growth rate and urged a step up in personnel recruiting quotas. But the operating people considered the forecast too optimistic and did not staff up for it. The result: a serious personnel squeeze when the new work began to pour in.

Also, any adopted objectives or goals should be reviewed from time to time and modified to meet changing conditions. Some areas of service that were once shunned by accountants as being unprofitable or unproductive could become more attractive in the future. Government work is an example. Audits of cities and municipalities by independent accountants are coming into greater vogue at the time of this writing. New York City's loss of financial credibility as the result of its budget shenanigans in the mid-1970s has shaken up many other city administrations. And the accounting profession is now concentrating on this new market.

TIGHTENING UP THE ORGANIZATION

There are certain basic attributes that a firm must have to merit acceptance in the marketplace. Without these, sustained growth simply will not occur, no matter what promotional techniques are adopted, or to what degree they are carried out. Indeed, otherwise effective communications techniques will actually speed the demise of an inferior product or organization by simply exposing its deficiencies to the marketplace. Having a favorable image to project is half the battle in a successful marketing program. The basic prerequisites include:

A Strong and Efficient Organization. Business people admire a fine organization whenever they find it. And they expect to find it in their accounting firm. Accounting firms should be organized to operate smoothly and efficiently and to last indefinitely.

Adequate Geographic Coverage. Clients look to their accountants to meet their service requirements wherever they may go—around the world, if necessary. While providing multi–office service coverage may not be of concern to a small firm serving local clients, the firms serving larger clients must keep up with the clients' expansion by providing appropriate office coverage in the U.S. and abroad.

A Complete Product or Service Line. While the attest function, auditing, is still the most distinctive service rendered by professional accountants, the special services—tax services, financial planning, systems, and the various management advisory services—have greater client appeal. The special service needs of clients should be anticipated and the necessary competencies acquired. Providing one–stop shopping is as relevant to an accounting firm as it is to a chain store. A professional accountant should not force his client to look to another accountant for services he should provide. Not only is it unprofessional, but he *could* lose the client!

Technical Competence and Quality. These are essential in any profession—and every professional must take whatever steps are necessary to assure high competence and quality. Some firms provide continuous training and quality control programs. The AICPA conducts an extensive professional development program. And professional literature can aid in keeping on top of current developments. But, ultimately, quality depends on the exercise of care, prudence, and judgment by each individual on every assignment.

Special Industry Competence. This is discussed in Chapter 11, The Industry Markets.

Competitive Fees. The decision to engage one accountant over another is rarely based on price alone, but every accountant or firm should keep fees reasonably competitive. Accountants should not sustain a loss in their work or attempt to "buy" an engagement by grossly underbidding; however, neither should they gouge. The fee structure should be based on costs and volume, with provision for fair compensation and return for the principals. Efficiency in performing client work and administering the practice is important too, if a firm is to remain competitive.

Dedication to Service. The entire accounting organization and everyone in it should be inspired with the idea that their business is client service—generous, willing, unstinting, prompt, helpful, and effective client service. The essence of professional services is sensing, serving, and satisfying client needs. This should be reflected in any marketing effort.

CHAPTER 14

The Marketing Department

WHAT IT DOES

The marketing department of a professional accounting firm organizes programs and directs activities designed to retain existing clients and attract new ones by sensing their needs, and satisfying them by delivering paid services in a manner consistent with prevailing professional precepts.

Thus the marketing department collects data and intelligence concerning the needs and opportunities in the markets for accounting services; it evaluates the firm's capacity to meet those needs; and it develops programs to bring the two together.

However, unlike the marketing division of a commercial or industrial organization, which invariably includes a sales force, the marketing department of a professional firm does not sell. It is a support function. It operates through a network of "marketing partners" who are located in each office or practice unit, and who direct and assist other partners and professional staff in local marketing activities. The marketing department also operates through the network of industry specialist groups. (See Chapter 11, The Industry Markets.)

The department furnishes behind–the–scenes ideas, direction, and support to those professionals who come into contact with new business opportunities in the ordinary course of their work or in other marketplaces in which they are active. It instructs them on how to gain favorable visibility in those marketplaces, and how to recognize business opportunities and convert them into new clients or engagements. (See Part I—THE BASICS OF SELLING PROFESSIONAL SERVICES.) It furnishes them with "sales tools"—directories and other publications that convey important information about the firm and its services. And it assists in preparing proposals and presentations for major engagements, particularly when other firms have also been invited to submit proposals.

The marketing department also directs public relations activities at the firm level—cultivating press and media relationships, preparing and distributing press releases, and helping with press conferences and interviews.

Thus, the department can be said to be engaged in administration, training, research, and communications.

In all its activities the marketing department should observe the prevailing ethics norms of the profession, particularly those relating to solicitation and advertising. While endeavoring to preserve the traditional professional image, the ethics rules and interpretations in effect at the time of this writing are not unduly restrictive and should not inhibit a wholesome marketing approach.

Finally, the marketing department should, of course, maintain a system for measuring the results of marketing programs and reporting on progress usually by practice unit, type of service, or market—for example, by industries or listed companies.

The Marketing Department's Place in the Organization

Becaue of its undoubted importance to a firm, marketing should be accorded a status in the organization equivalent to that of the important practice functions. Ideally, the director of marketing should be a seasoned CPA and a ranking partner. He should be knowledgeable in all aspects of marketing and skilled in communications. He should have a record of attracting and clinching new clients. And if he has an outstanding professional reputation as a result of authoritative writings or lectures on accounting or related subjects, so much the better.

The head of marketing should report directly to the chief executive partner of the firm. And, regardless of whether his department is part of the firm's line or staff organization (it probably should be the latter), he should have direct access to all offices and personnel.

The department probably ought to be called what it is—marketing. There has been a tendency in the past to obscure the marketing function in accounting firms by calling them practice development or some similarly bland title and otherwise relegating their activities to the back room. Undoubtedly this was thought desirable to preserve a professional image in a more genteel era. But the obfuscation seems hardly necessary in today's more candid environment. Deborah Rankin observed in a 1977 *New York Times* article, "How CPA's Sell Themselves:"

> The Accountants insist on referring to their efforts to drum up business as "practice development." But many of the activities that fall under this euphemism are dead ringers for what is called "marketing" in other fields . . .
>
> Indeed, within the halls of the strait–laced accounting profession, where one might think the liveliest topic of conversation would be the relative merits of LIFO versus FIFO, the talk now is filled with marketing jargon. Accountants speak of "positioning" their firms and of "penetrating" unexploited new industries. They compile "hit lists" of prospective clients and then "surround" them by placing their firms' partners in close social contact with the top executives of target companies.

According the marketing function the same status that it enjoys in commercial establishments would have the added benefit of permitting marketing people—editors, writers, and communicators—to come out of the back room and enjoy the visibility and recognition merited by their role and talents.

DETERMINING MARKET NEEDS AND OPPORTUNITIES

Aside from mergers with other firms, an accounting firm has three principal sources of growth: existing clients, special services, and new clients. Monitoring the developments and opportunities in the markets for these and evaluating the firm's capacity to meet them is an important part of the marketing effort.

Responding to the Growth of Existing Clients

While there is comparatively little growth potential in, say, individual income tax clients, institutional and business clients—particularly the latter—tend to grow over the years. Volumes increase, product lines multiply, and geographic locations fan out. The growth may originate from within the business itself, or it may be the result of an acquisition or merger with another business.

Whatever the reasons for their growth, expanding clients require expanded auditing services, expecially when they "go public" and become subject to SEC filing requirements. And their increased size and complexity frequently call for more sophisticated tax planning and management services as well—particularly in the areas of systems and controls.

Keeping alert to such developments on both a short– and long–term basis is a function of marketing—particularly when client needs increase faster than the accounting firm's capacity to satisfy them. If the clients' expanded geographic needs, for example, cannot economically be served from the firm's existing offices, some action is required. The firm may find it desirable to establish an office in a new location— particularly if there is already enough client work in that area to support a balanced staff. Or the firm may decide it should absorb the expenses of staff travel to the distant location until such time as the volume of accounting work there would warrant a new office. But the needs of growing clients must be met, if the accounting firm is to grow. Many local firms were literally forced to merge with national firms in the 1950s and 1960s, because they stood by while their clients' needs expanded faster than their capacity to serve them.

Analyzing Special Services Markets and Opportunities

Clients' needs in the special services areas are also expanding constantly, and, of course, new techniques and competencies are always developing within the services themselves.

Electronic data processing consulting is an example of a service that developed within the past two decades. Most of the large accounting firms have responded to this post–World War II innovation by acquiring technicians at the systems analysts level. Indeed, a few actually took on programmers and undertook programming engagements.

Another comparatively new service was international tax consulting services. U.S. companies contemplating foreign expansion in the 1950s and 1960s desperately required information concerning foreign tax systems and rates and their interrelationship with provisions of the Federal income tax. Foreign tax "havens" or "sanctuaries" became the vogue. But even the so–called international accounting firms had to undertake extensive research to acquire the knowledge to meet this new demand.

Medicare audits of hospitals and nursing homes, which developed in the late 1960s, also represented a vast new area of service.

And the expanded accounting, auditing, and reporting requirements for pension plans under the new ERISA law has spawned still another new area of service.

At the time of this writing the Department of Health, Education, and Welfare is considering accepting audits by independent accountants of federally sponsored activities of universities—those for which the university is reimbursed under federal grants and contracts. Ordinarily, the federal government conducts its own audits of the university programs it sponsors, but because of staff shortages it has not been able to keep up with the requisite audits.

Keeping abreast of special service demands and gearing the firm to meet them is an important marketing exercise.

Directing Activities in New Client Markets

Keeping in touch with the markets for new audit clients is somewhat more difficult, for, as indicated earlier, the sources of new audit clients are many and varied and require a multifaceted approach.

Some professional marketing people seem to believe that every business in the community is fair game for the service firm and should be solicited on a methodical basis. This simply would not be appropriate for professional accountants—even if it were not specifically prohibited by the Code of Ethics.

Most businesses have auditors, and it is almost impossible to unseat them in the absence of dissatisfaction. The "catch" from such a "shotgun" approach would be nil. Also, professional accountants do not have the time to devote to full–blown sales campaigns—nor can the task be turned over to laymen. And the independence of the auditor, if he is ultimately appointed as such, is bound to suffer if he has stooped too low for the engagement.

Rather, emphasis should be placed on identifying the appropriate marketplaces; appearing regularly, participating actively, and becoming favorably known in those marketplaces; staying alert to the opportunities *that present themselves;* and being trained to convert those opportunities into new clients—all without relinquishing one's natural dignity or professional attitude.

Under the circumstances, then, the central marketing function selects those forums or arenas that offer the greatest potential for gaining new clients, assigns appropriate partners and staff to those markets, and coaches them on how to recognize an opportunity and convert it into a new client.

This is a rifle approach. It works. And it is considerably more efficient and productive than the cold canvass of an amorphous universe of disparate businesses.

The marketplaces and forums are cited herein—they

include industry associations, general business and trade organizations, civic associations, and many others. (See Part III—Accountancy's Markets and Its Publics)

DEVELOPING AN INFORMATION AND INTELLIGENCE BASE

While the marketing function in commercial enterprises looks outside for much of its information and intelligence, particularly that relating to the marketplace, it usually finds that the principal source of data is its own organization. In most cases it is an ongoing product of the organization's financial reporting system. It is the type of thing that capable management uses to monitor month to month operations—reports of sales and profits by product, department, and class of customer, for example. These reports are produced in the ordinary course of business. But they are particularly useful to the marketing people in policy formulation and decision–making. If the sales of a particular product or division were to sag, for example, the marketing people would want to know this promptly in order to determine the cause of the problem and correct it.

There are other types of internal data that are not normally a product of an organization's financial reporting system, but which are nonetheless essential to the marketing function. One example: listings of new customers and how they were obtained. Or, listings of customers lost and why they were lost.

Most of the statistical data required by the professional accounting firm's marketing function is also an ongoing product of the firm's accounting department or other internal sources. It includes:

Departmental Operating Information. The internal operating statements of an accounting firm usually report volume, expenses, profits, and profit ratios for each office or practice unit in terms of dollars and man–hours, both by type of service and industry class. In itself, such data can help immensely in making marketing decisions—for example, in whether to stress particularly profitable types of services. And knowing the profitability of work performed in various industry classes can be extremely helpful in formulating marketing strategy. Invariably, government work will prove to be the least profitable, simply because of the intense price competition that is engendered by the government bidding process. The desirability of pursuing such work at a low profit margin can be rationalized, of course, as a means of absorbing overhead or even as an acknowledgment of a firm's responsibility to its government. But this is a typical marketing decision that is made possible only by having available profit data by client or class.

Special Industry Competence. Along with the information that is usually contained in personnel files might be added references to specialized industry competence or experience of the persons involved. This can prove especially helpful when writing a proposal or staffing a new client engagement in an unfamiliar industry. The industry approach to organizing and conducting an accounting practice and the types of data that are required are spelled out in Chapter 11, The Industry Markets.

Client Information. The central client file can be one of the most important sources of marketing data. Among other things, it might contain information concerning the client's size, location, stock exchange listing, and industry class, as well as similar data concerning any affiliates or subsidiaries. In addition, the files might include the names and addresses of officers and directors and any other affiliations. General and selective mailings to these people can only strengthen the bond between an accounting firm and its clients.

Clients Gained and Lost. An important by–product of client file updating is monthly reports of clients gained or lost, along with the estimated fees involved. Summarized by class of service, industry, and location, these can provide an ongoing measure of the results of the firm's marketing efforts from month–to–month or year–to–year.

Information on the sources of new clients and the reasons for client losses, of course, is particularly vital in formulating marketing programs. One of the principal sources of new clients, for example, is recommendations by existing clients. Another is referrals by lawyers. Marketing people need to be aware of these when designing communications pieces. Incidentally, client losses are frequently attributed to "fee problems," when, in fact, the real cause is usually dissatisfaction with the services rendered or the treatment received!

The mere production and examination of these several types of information by an accounting firm is in itself a giant step toward embracing the marketing concept. The simple dissemination of the information to firm personnel is bound to inspire ideas and actions that will spur increased volume and profits.

Data from Outside Sources–Listed Companies

The marketing function also needs information from *outside* sources, particularly data concerning the firm's markets and its competitors. New York Stock Exchange–listed companies, for example, constitute a major market for accounting firms. And large firms have for years measured their shares of this market vis–a–vis those of competitor firms, by regularly tabulating the auditors of companies listed on the Big Board—information that incidentally is now available in the commercial publication *Who Audits America*.

Another approach to comparing market shares is to tabulate principal companies and their auditors by industry. This will reveal a surprising predominance of some auditing firms in certain industries.

As suggested earlier, more aggressive firms give special attention to the large companies they do *not* audit by identifying top officers and cultivating them through social club mem-

berships and other means. Their objective: to be thought
of favorably in case a change in auditors is to be made.

Accumulating information concerning potential clients
and staying alert to opportunities to be of service is, of
course, a typical marketing exercise—although traditionalists
no doubt will continue to insist that auditors' independence is
threatened by overt efforts to develop relationships with officials of companies they may be engaged to audit. This may
be so, but any such threat would seem fairly innocuous when
compared to the really tough moral problems that the accountant is coping with today.

Moreover, as pointed out before, accounting firms have
been fiercely competitive for at least 15 years. And while they
may not have solicited the clients of other firms, they certainly have pursued all other avenues to make themselves
known to non–clients in a favorable light. There is no indication that audit independence is weakened by this practice.

Listed companies, or indeed publicly owned companies,
are not the only potential market for accounting firms, although they undoubtedly represent the largest single one.
The hundreds of thousands of privately owned businesses
and institutions also comprise a significant market. These,
too, are sometimes staked out as potential clients by accounting firms on a local or regional basis and assigned to particular partners or staff for cultivation on a regular basis. Sometimes the assigned partner or staff member is required to
report on actions taken or progress made in the cultivation
process. These reports, of course, are akin to salesmen's "call
reports" in a commercial establishment.

Marketing people must preside over many other information assemblies as well. Like the driver on the freeway,
they must be completely aware of everything that is going on
around them.

The Image Survey

An accounting firm suffering from lack of growth in com-
parison with other firms no doubt would wish to determine

exactly how it stands with its publics before evolving its marketing program or designing communications pieces. A good hard look at its image can be helpful. This can be done by the firm's partners or by independent survey people. Staff members and other employees of the firm should be among those queried in the survey—and they should be guaranteed anonymity in order to encourage them to discuss any negative impressions they may have.

Chances are the survey will not reveal any serious deficiencies in the quality, variety, or accessibility of the firm's services vis–a–vis those offered by other firms—although it may. If so, these should be corrected. During the late 1950s and early 1960s, for example, a number of firms found themselves lagging behind the competition in such areas as foreign office coverage and types of consulting services offered. And they suffered a competitive disadvantage until they filled the gaps in their international coverage and rounded out their service lines.

Actually, the problems unearthed in a survey of a firm's standing with its publics will often be found to be communications–related. Clients frequently complain, for example, that auditors are in such a hurry to leave after completing the audit they do not take the time to discuss their ancillary findings. Clients, of course, are as interested in the auditors' observations concerning the overall conduct and direction of the business as they are in comments on the accounts or internal controls. The failure to take the time and trouble to discuss these is a breakdown in communications.

The need to maintain effective communications with clients deserves the highest priority in a marketing program, not only to forestall possible erosion, but because satisfied clients beget new clients. A tabulation by one large accounting firm of the sources of new clients revealed that over 50% were referred or recommended by existing clients. Referrals by lawyers and other professionals and personal contacts of partners and staff accounted for 15% each. Surprisingly, banks turned out to be a remarkably poor source of new business for that firm. But clients were by far the greatest single source.

The attitudes and needs of clients and, indeed, all the firm's publics should be pinned down before communications pieces are developed, for if they are developed without regard to their intended audiences, they will surely miss the mark.

PROVIDING TRAINING IN COMMUNICATIONS

By far the most productive activity of a central marketing function is to train firm people in communications—how to speak, how to write, what to say, and how to make a presentation. (See Chapter 3, Learning to Communicate Effectively.) For experience has proven time and time again that, given the requisite technical knowledge and expertise, the selection of one professional over another is invariably motivated by the receipt of a confidence–communication by the prospect. This depends on the professional's capacity to transmit within the receiver's range of perception. Thus the development of a professional practice depends largely on the presence of communications abilities in individual professionals. Training in this area is probably the most economical area in which to commit marketing dollars.

Some firms provide public speaking and writing courses for their professional people. Others provide instruction for the making of effective presentations to potential clients.

There are many commerical courses and audio–visual packages available for such instruction. One custom made film utilizing a well–known TV newscaster as the principal narrator cited the steps necessary for clinching a new client and applied these in a simulated new client presentation based on an actual case. The use of this film over a relatively short period of time resulted in a marked increase in the particular firm's new client clinching rate.

A custom made film, of course, has an advantage over commercial films in that it can refer to actual facts, people, and situations. And if done artfully enough, it will stimulate the professionals who are exposed to it to emulate the presentation, even to the point of using the exact words!

CHAPTER 15

The Communications Function
–Types of Communications and
Messages

The accounting profession got along in its first 60 years without recognizing any particular need for organized, systematic client communications. CPAs generally were engaged in auditing or tax work, and their practices were not so big that communications with clients suffered. Even the larger firms were not too large to maintain effective communications in person, or by letter or telephone. Nor were the technical changes in their lore so vital or so numerous that they required prompt communication. About all that happened were intermittent changes in the tax law.

The post–World War II explosion in accounting developments, tax changes, and management technology, however, expanded the need for information by clients and called for an effective means of disseminating it promptly. And businesses expanded geographically throughout the United States and abroad, creating new needs for different types of information.

U.S. business' migration abroad in the late 1950s, for example, created a need for data on accounting conventions and tax laws in various foreign countries. Accounting firms were looked to for much of this, and some accounting firms responded to the need for technical information on doing business abroad by compiling it in formal technical memoranda and booklets for client use.

Management systems, methods, procedures, and techniques also improved substantially during this period, as did the applications of data processing equipment. Businesses were compelled by competition alone to stay abreast of these developments. With their relatively new management services competencies now in place, accounting firms began to make use of this information by assembling, and regularly communicating it to their clients and others.

And, of course, there were the increasing "marketing" needs of accountants and their firms—the need to develop and maintain work in an even flow.

Accounting firms began to step up their communications with clients and other *direct* publics around 1960. Their publications now serve both their clients' needs for technical information and their own need for marketing visibility and exposure. But it took professional communicators to get them on the track.

ENTER THE COMMUNICATORS

The acceptance of marketing and public relations concepts (see Chapter 16, Public Relations Aspects) led to the employment of professional–level writers and graphics people by accounting firms, and the organization of central communications divisions. Headed by a director of communications or a managing editor reporting to the Director of Marketing, such a division designs and produces the printed and other publications that are the backbone of a firm's marketing and public relations programs. While, as pointed out in Chapter 16, the two programs may emphasize different publics, there is much overlap. Indeed, with the possible exception of press releases which have only one destination, the press, most communications are interchangeable and can support both the marketing and public relations efforts. In fact, the two functions are considered indistinguishable by communications people.

Communicators tend to classify an accounting firm's

publications by whether they are for internal or external audiences; by media—for example, print, audio-visual, or electronic; and by mode of communication, such as books, pamphlets or newsletters; or slides, film strips, or videotapes. They classify messages or content by subject categories; for example, technical, international, industrial, or socio–economic.

The ultimate effectiveness of a communication depends upon the intrinsic interest of the message to its intended audience and the artistry or skill of the communicator.

While all true communicators are endowed with imagination and creativity and a desire to express themselves, their effectiveness depends upon the rigorousness of their training in their basic art or craft—in writing, speaking, drawing, painting, or music—and the breadth of their experience.

The communicator has become important in today's society. Dr. Marshall McLuhan, the high priest of communications, suggests that he will become even more influential as a greater proportion of the population becomes involved in assembling and transporting information. He notes that "the artist is today shifting from the Ivory Tower to the Control Tower; no nation, no business can navigate now without the vision of the artist."

While originally distrusting communicators, accountants have learned that their integrity and skills match their own. Even medium–sized and small firms are increasingly engaging writers or graphics people sometimes on a free lance basis to assist with communications projects; for example, to design and produce a directory or brochure. Certainly every firm of more than five people should include one who is at least moderately skilled in writing. Most larger firms are finding it worthwhile to engage a full–time writer. As McLuhan said, no business can navigate without an artist.

TYPES OF COMMUNICATIONS AND MEDIA

For purposes of convenience, the communications of an accounting firm can be said to fall into four categories:

Speeches and Other Oral Communications
External Publications for Clients and Other External Publics and
    Audiences
Internal Publications for Professional Personnel
Press Placements and Publicity

Speeches and Other Oral Communications

Except for providing an occasional model speech for the
neophyte, or assisting in writing or editing a speech to be
delivered by an experienced professional, the communications department ordinarily has little contact with oral communications. As pointed out in Chapter 3, Learning to
Communicate Effectively, speeches and other oral communications are exclusively the province of the individual
accountant. The Communications Division can furnish him
with information and ideas. It can also supply aids in the
form of printed pieces or charts or audio visual material.
And it can even monitor his presentation in order to help
him become more effective. But it cannot make his speech or
oral presentation for him. That is uniquely a personal communication.   ·

The professional accountant's potential audiences and
listeners are described in Chapter 4, Forums for Gaining
Visibility, and Chapter 12, The Publics. They include:

Clients' management and other personnel.
Prospective clients' managements.
Boards of directors and trustees.
Stockholders' meetings.
Professional and technical seminars.
Industry association meetings.
Business, trade, and civic organization meetings.
University seminars and symposiums.
Congressional and other legislative hearings.
Press interviews and conferences.

External Publications

The Mailing List. Since external publications are distributed principally by mail, mailing lists need to be developed

and maintained. And since client officers and other personnel are to be the principal recipients of these publications,
the firm's central client files are a natural source of the initial
mailing list, as well as subsequent additions and deletions.
Most firms update their client files at least once a year, usually while conducting the annual audit, and this process can
also be used to update mailing lists and keep them fresh.

A mailing list should be personalized—it should contain
names of persons, not companies. If the mailing address is to
be the company's office, the person's title should follow his
name, viz,

> Joseph J. Jones, Executive Vice President
> The Manor Corporation
> 2 Broadway
> New York, N.Y. 10004

Worthwhile publications should practically never be addressed to a company or organization per se, for, like pamphlets addressed to "resident" or "occupant," they become
cheapened and lose most of their intended impact.

In addition to client personnel, mailing lists should also
include the names of others with whom the firm wishes to
communicate—bankers, lawyers, educators, and government
officials, for example. (See Chapter 12, The Publics.) These
sections of the mailing list are more difficult to develop and
maintain than the client section, because contact is often intermittent and spasmodic. The source of these names should
be partners and other firm personnel—they should be
people who are known to the firm. And these listings should
also be reviewed at least annually to determine whether the
personal relationships still warrant the continued inclusion
of the names.

Ideally, the central mailing list should be classified by
types of clients and publics so that the various types of publications or bulletins can be directed only to those readers who
will have the greatest interest in the contents or messages.
Individual income tax clients, for example, are not likely to
be interested in foreign accounting developments, but would

surely be interested in a new type of tax shelter. Naturally, compartmentalization of the mailing list should not be carried too far. One of the purposes of the publications program is to demonstrate a firm's breadth, and recipients should be able to gain that impression from a simple scanning of the table of contents or the story headings themselves.

For this reason, an omnibus publication that ranges across a variety of subjects and contains something of interest for everyone can be extremely effective. It should contain a quick reference summary so that items of particular interest can be easily spotted by the reader. A monthly client newsletter is an example of an omnibus publication.

But first, there should be a firm directory—if the firm is big enough to warrant such a publication.

Firm Directory. A firm directory is usually the single most important outside publication a firm can undertake. Its graphics design alone, if tastefully done, can convey such positive attitudes as dynamism, progressiveness, and willingness to serve. The directory should portray the firm's overall organization and its various service departments and office locations, along with the names of partners and other professional personnel and their positions in the organization.

A directory can be as useful to people within a firm as it is in revealing the firm to its clients. For it serves as a reference. Moreover, the mere act of assembling a directory can result in significant improvements in the substance of the firm's organization. The first attempt to draft an organization chart for inclusion in the directory, for example, can reveal any gaps, holes, or ambiguities in the organization. Sometimes these are a result of management indecision or delay—such as the failure to designate a successor in charge of a particular function or unit or to prescribe clear lines of authority and accountability. While possibly tolerable within the firm itself, such infirmities cry for correction before the firm's organization is revealed to the outside. The directory thus becomes a focal point for detecting and resolving structural weaknesses in the organization, and in the process it assumes a distinctive stature of its own.

Newsletters and Bulletins. An attractively designed, well–written monthly client letter or bulletin can be extremely effective in maintaining relations with clients and other publics. It can serve as an ongoing "voice" of a firm.

A newsletter should be distributed to a firm's professional personnel, as well as to its external audiences. For not only will they find it useful and informative; they also should be kept apprised of what the firm is saying to its clients. Partners and staff should be encouraged to scan the contents promptly so as not to be taken by surprise by a client's comments or questions.

A newsletter should convey a firm's position on any important or controversial developments in accounting, auditing, and financial reporting. Indeed, the desirability of making its position known to its clients in an early issue of the letter will sometimes nudge a firm into arriving at a decision over which it might otherwise vacillate indefinitely.

A newsletter should report important developments in taxes and management methods and techniques for the continual education of those within a firm, and to afford "new product" visibility to clients.

The letter might report on and analyze general developments in business and commerce, as well as economics and government, and so broaden the perspective of those within the firm while conveying an impression of breadth to those outside. This can help to negate the image of accountants as narrow technicians.

The letter might also include valuable information or compendia for use by both internal and external audiences—for example, tabulations of year end foreign exchange rates that can be useful to clients engaged in foreign operations.

Certainly, a monthly letter or bulletin should report important developments within a firm, in service innovations or new office locations, for example, as well as unusual honors or appointments conferred on firm people.

It should announce the availability of other firm publications to its readers. Indeed, the volume of responses to offerings of new publications can provide some indication of how well the newsletter is perused by its intended readers—although a better method of measuring readership interest is by direct questionnaires to readers eliciting their views and suggestions.

Naturally, it is almost impossible for every issue of a periodical to be better than the one before. But a high general standard of content and presentation can be maintained in such a publication. Certainly it can be kept fresh and timely by intermittent changes in layout or format, even to the extent of occasionally changing the type face or redesigning the masthead.

One way to achieve high quality in a periodical is to put an experienced professional editor in charge and carry his name on the masthead. His sense of professional pride will usually assure a quality publication. The practice of identifying professional editors and writers with their product is becoming more prevalent, not only in private publications, but in commercial newspapers and magazines as well. *Barron's, Wall Street Journal* and *New York Times* have long identified their writers with their stories. And even *Newsweek* and *Time* are moving in that direction—an acknowledgment of the growing stature of communicators.

Magazines and Other External Publications. Some accounting firms issue magazines and journals containing by–lined articles on accounting and related subjects by partners and staff, profiles of prestigious clients or universities from which the firm obtains or hopes to obtain promising recruits, reports on speeches and other activities of firm people, biographies of new partners, births and deaths, and other internal intelligence. These journals are usually replete with photos, charts, and other graphics of extremely high quality. Indeed, magazines of several of the large firms compare favorably in graphics and format with the best of commercial magazines. Since some of these firm journals started as house organs as long as 50 years ago and were only recently modified for external audiences as well, they tend to convey a certain quaintness and warmth that is not lost on the outside reader.

The Battle of the Recruiting Brochures. The height of graphics elegance, however, seems to have been reserved for recruiting brochures—particularly those of the major firms. Their principal purpose, that of attracting promising college graduates, is not circumscribed by ethics prohibitions. Thus all the pent–up creative merchandising energies that might have gone into the more restricted new business brochures have apparently been channeled into the recruiting brochures. The brochures of the various Big Twelve Firms are truly handsome four color global presentations of the firms and their services. They compare favorably with the most elegant recruiting brochures of the major industrial companies competing for the same accounting graduates. While all the brochures are no doubt eagerly read by the graduates, it is likely that their ultimate selection of employer is influenced more by the personalities and persuasiveness of the respective recruiters than by the brochures themselves. But the brochures have their value, if no more than to uphold the firm's competitive standing in the highly visible brochure rack in the college placement office.

Also, while aimed principally at accounting graduates, these brochures have proven equally useful in making new client presentations as well.

Other external publications appropriate for accounting firms include monographs on technical subjects and copies or reprints of by–lined articles written by firm personnel that have appeared elsewhere. Hard–bound books written by partners and staff and published by commercial publishers are also frequently purchased in quantity by accounting firms and distributed to clients and friends.

In sum, accounting firms are using just about every form of printed publication to keep their publics informed of technical developments and to pursue their own marketing aims.

Internal Publications

While external publications of an accounting firm are usually intended for the members of its own organization, as well as for clients and other outsiders, there are certain types of publications that are appropriate only for internal personnel. These include materials for training partners and staff in selling and marketing techniques, and internal bulletins or newsletters that periodically report the results of the firm's marketing activities—that is, names of new clients, special engagements obtained, and by whom, and ideas and suggestions for improving performance.

The internal publications also include descriptions of the various classes of services rendered by the firm in a form that aids partners and staff to articulate them to others.

Information Primers and Directories. Without thinking about it beforehand, most accountants would find it difficult to describe their work to non-accountants. And yet the building of a practice requires an accountant to be able to describe what he does and what others in his firm do, in clear and consise lay terms. A tax specialist, for example, might be inclined to say, "I do tax work," when a description like the following would convey infinitely more information and make a considerably better impression:

"I specialize in taxes—principally income taxes. I work with our audit staff in verifying the provisions for federal and state taxes that our business clients set up for financial statement purposes. I prepare income tax returns for individuals and corporations. I deal with revenue agents when they examine the returns; and I prepare protests against additional assessments and represent the taxpayer in hearings and conferences before the Internal Revenue Service people. The most creative thing I do, though, is to help clients with financial and tax planning. I advise them on the tax effects of proposed transactions, and sometimes suggest alternative arrangements for achieving the same objective at a lower tax cost. I also call their attention to various tax shelter opportunities like deferred annuities—that sort of thing."

An orderly presentation of the various services offered by the firm is particularly helpful in apprising the members of one discipline about the services of the others; for example, familiarizing the auditor with what the management consultant does and vice versa so that both can describe their colleagues' work to others.

The names of significant clients of the firm classified by location and industry is still another type of basic information that should be made accessible, particularly when a firm has a number of offices. Partners and staff are sometimes not aware of prestigious clients who are served by other offices of their firm. And since companies tend to lean towards the accounting firms that serve others in their industry, having client information at one's fingertips can prove important in attracting and clinching clients.

Directories of professional personnel are also important communications. These usually include photographs and personal and professional data about each partner and principal, including home address and phone number, wife's name, schools attended, committee memberships and chairmanships in professional organizations, authorships, and special industry competence. Such listings are difficult to assemble and maintain—pictures particularly have a way of getting out of date, especially high school graduation photos. However these compilations of information do facilitate communications within the firm and add to the cohesiveness of the organization.

Training Materials. Materials for instructing or training partners and staff in selling techniques include booklets containing the type of information described in Chapter 5, Retaining Present Clients Etc., or films that simulate a new client presentation. (See page 144).

Since partners and staff are the firm's principal representatives and spokesmen in the marketplace, anything that can help them increase their effectiveness is worthwhile. This includes up–to–date information about the firm and its services and instruction in selling and marketing techniques.

Press Releases and Publicity (See Chapter 16)

While commercial enterprises customarily seek publicity by issuing a large volume of press releases concerning innovations and developments, accounting firms find it more appropriate to set up informal background meetings with members of the press, from which appropriate stories ensue more naturally. Their purpose is to make the press more aware of the complexities of the issues that are faced by the profession and its members—the problems in prescribing hard and fast accounting principles and in making value judgments in grey areas. These briefings often emphasize the judgmental and skill aspects of accounting and the fact that it is not as amenable to a cookbook approach as is popularly thought—even by sophisticated people.

This and other forms of publicity are covered in Chapter 16, Public Relations Aspects—The Press.

THE MESSAGE—EXAMPLES

Upon receiving the first issue of his firm's new client newsletter sometime ago, one of the partners observed to the editor, "The new publication is certainly attractive and interesting;

but how do you expect to keep it going—there just isn't enough happening to warrant a monthly publication." The remark was made 20 years ago. The particular newsletter has appeared regularly ever since—an indication of the limitless depths of ideas, events, and imagination.

Actually, the messages accountants and firms communicate to their clients and friends are as voluminous and varied as imagination itself. Here are some examples selected at random from the thousands of titles that have appeared in publications of various firms:

Internal Intelligence

Highlight Listing of Recent New Clients
Managing Partner Accorded High Honor
New Partners Admitted to Firm
New Industry Specialists Appointed
Insurance Specialists Merge With Firm
New Office Opened in Dunmore
Government Expert Joins MCS Group
Personnel Transfers
Interesting Engagements—With Practice Development Implications
Furthering Our Financial Industry Practice
Cost Reduction Program Hikes Client Earnings
Client Uses Staff Course Manual as Internal Auditing Tool
Phase II Seminars Draw Strong Client Response
Behind the Scenes in Firm's Tax Practice
Economy and the Firm's Practice in Germany

Technical Intelligence

CASB: That Other Accounting Standards Board
Accountants Win More Cases—Has the Tide Changed?
Investment Planning With Tax Exempt Bonds
Valuation of Closely Held Corporate Stock
Are Auditors Responsible for Fraud Detection
Accounting Regulatory Bodies: Pronouncements and Rules
Replacement Cost—Price Level Accounting from Management's Point of View
New Tax Act Provisions

Special Industry Commentaries

The Audit Committee: A Working Guide for Audit Committee
Members of a *Retail Organization*
Productivity Improvement Manual for *Local Government* Officials
Financial Reporting and Accounting Practices of *Private Founda-
tions*
Audit Proposals for *Insurance Companies*
Curriculum for the *College* Crisis
Tallying the Tall *Timbers*
Management Accounting for *Hospitals*
A Study of the 1973 Annual Reports of the Hundred Largest
Commercial Banks
Accounting for *Condominium* Sales
Survey of Accounting and Reporting Practices of *Real Estate De-
velopers*
Financial Survey of the *Soft Drink Industry*
U.S. *Lodging* Industry—Study of Investor Owned *Hospitals*
Insurance—Tax Relief May be Available to Companies That Sus-
tained Abnormal Losses in 1974

General Business Commentaries

The Corporate Accountability System Under Fire
Business Ethics
The Emerging Revolution in Electronic Payments
Annual Meetings—Questions from Shareholders
Executive Compensation
Checklist—Hospital Trustee Responsibilities
Privacy Laws—Business Should Act Now to Influence Outcome
of Extending Privacy Laws to Commercial Sector

International

Individual Taxes in 80 Countries
Accounting Principles and Reporting Practices in 46 Countries
Credit Conditions Abroad
Foreign Exchange Summary
Foreign Trade Support Organizations
Social Security Pacts with Foreign Countries
U.S.-U.K. Tax Treaty Would Lower Dividend Taxes
India—New Tax Incentive Aimed at Stimulating Business De-
velopment
Iran—Trade Opportunities Abound in Middle East

CHAPTER 16

Public Relations Aspects
–The Press

While the marketing and public relations functions are often independent of each other in commercial enterprises, they are virtually inseparable in a professional accounting firm. They can be distinguished from each other in only one important aspect, the publics they seek to reach and the media they use to reach them.

Marketing concentrates on many specific markets and sub-markets. It seeks to expand the firm's services and clientele. It emphasizes the specific advantages and benefits of these services to the buyers or users. And it conveys its message to specific audiences by word of mouth or through limited printed and audio visual communications.

Public relations, on the other hand, deals with the vast amorphous public at large. It seeks to win public understanding and support for an organization, its people, and its works. It emphasizes the contributions of the firm and its services to the broad socio–economic community. It conveys its message principally through news stories or other unpaid publicity in mass media—newspapers and magazines, as well as radio and television.

In short, marketing deals with products or services—and public relations with attitudes.

PUBLIC RELATIONS PROCEDURES

Ideally, the public relations function seeks to gain and hold public acceptance by continuous ongoing programs. It formulates a public relations platform or policy. It analyzes the organization's philosophy, policies, and standards and endeavors to conform them to broad public needs, demands, and expectations. It seeks to channel the organization's resources and the energies of its people toward specific activities or programs in the public interest. It develops press releases and other pronouncements concerning these programs and activities; and it selects appropriate media and communicates its story or message.

The Handbook of Public Relations describes public relations procedures as "circular," since they begin and end with research. These include five steps, all of which are based on a defined platform of public relations policy:

Internal Research. The collection of information, impressions, and ideas within an organization. This builds up the wealth of basic material that the organization will use.

Integration with Policy. The application of judgment to make sure that every message furthers the public relations purpose.

Preparation of the Message. The process of conceptualizing and articulating the message, putting it in proper form for dissemination.

Communication. The process of delivering the message to the public via the appropriate media.

External Research. The appraisal of the extent to which the message has been understood, the effect it has had, and the nature of the public's reaction. It also classifies the public or audience by reference to attitudes.

The PR Fraternity

The public relations fraternity traces its antecedents to such pioneers as Ivey Lee, who worked to improve John D. Rockefeller Sr.'s public image in the early part of the century.

But strong impetus towards professionalization did not develop until the formation of The Public Relations Society of America in 1949. The Society established education and experience requirements for admission to its "active" category and prescribed a code of professional standards and behavior for public relations practitioners.

The public relations profession has already built an impressive body of knowledge, which is reflected in such works as the previously mentioned *Handbook of Public Relations,* an impressive 850 page reference, and many others.

Traditionally, public relations people are writers—journalism graduates or former newspaper writers. Recent PR literature suggests, however, that the concept of public relations may be broadening and its educational and experience requirements expanding. Jack Squire of Basford Public Relations has been quoted in the PR Journal as saying, "You see less and less demand for a newspaper background now and more demand for technical knowledge or expertise, general corporation or business experience, or political science or sociology backgrounds—people with good broad educations."

But the proud hard core of the public relations fraternity still envisage themselves primarily as writers and publicists and their product as press connections and publicity. They measure the success of their efforts by reference to the volume and types of publicity their clients or employers receive in the media. They hold the "efficient press" theory—that what the media says is what the public believes—and they can produce research studies to support this.

Communications skills are as basic to public relations people as adeptness with figures is to accountants. But just as accountancy requires that its members be steeped in the environment in which the figures reside, public relations requires that its practitioners be familiar with the environment in which their communications travel. For it too is a profession of substance, breadth, and integrity.

THE ACCOUNTANTS' NEGLECTED IMAGE

The accounting profession's long aversion to public relations and publicity has exceeded even its antipathy towards marketing. Here, too, a long–standing ethics precept was involved, one that forbade the seeking of publicity.

However, more likely, members of the profession shunned public relations because they did not generally appreciate the extent to which their work had become vested with the broad public interest. (See Chapter 7, Auditing's Changing Marketplace.) Nor did they seem to understand the power of public opinion or the importance of cultivating a positive public image. And they apparently did not perceive the erosion that was occurring in their image during the 1960s or feel the need for a sustained media program to clear that image. Even when hit by the blaze of unfavorable publicity in the late 1960s, the profession still seemed reluctant to move from the reserve of a semi–cloistered environment into the glare of the public spotlight.

The seeds for that media explosion of course were planted in the early 1960s, with charges from both within and without the profession that acccounting principles were not as well established or defined as the public thought them to be—and that a philosophically divided profession was apparently unable to do anything about it. This philosophic division, no doubt, represented a chink in the profession's armor that opened the breach for the series of court suits which followed.

These court actions, which ironically involved auditing standards more than accounting principles, alleged the failure of CPAs and their firms to detect or disclose vital information concerning companies whose statements they examined. A few involved criminal charges—and convictions.

The pendulum continued to swing against accountants in the late 1960s. Doubts were expressed about the CPA's independence and his ability to perform an objective audit of a company for which he performed management advisory services. Questions were raised concerning the scope of his audit—whether it goes far enough. Some felt that a CPA's audit should include a review and report on the efficiency of the company's operations and its management, as well as on its financial condition. With corporate ownership dispersed among millions of shareholders, the question of who checks on management assumed new importance.

The Profession's Standing in the Private Sector

The profession had not, of course, been standing still. While it may not have perceived the growing demands of the public at large, it certainly had expanded the scope and breadth of its services to meet many of the technical and geographic needs of those business organizations with which it had direct contact. And it later focused on the needs of eleemosynary institutions as well, including colleges and universities, hospitals, and governments. The results in terms of financial stability and improved productivity and profitability are well known. The profession had a good standing with its clients and with certain other limited publics, if for no other reason than the demonstrated value of its services in adding order to their particular economic activities. And, as pointed out in Chapter 6, the accountant has had a significant influence on the development of the largest capital market and most productive industrial complex ever.

General Public Not Aware of Accomplishments

But the *general public* was not aware of these developments or accomplishments. Few read technical journals or had direct contact with the profession or its members. The public knew little of the standards of competence and morality that prevailed in the profession generally and in its great firms. It was not aware of the nature or limitations of the attest function and probably would not have been impressed anyway—in view of its rapidly rising expectations. Indeed, it is quite likely that the general public's impressions of the CPA were gained largely from the mass media.

And there the CPA projected poorly!

As the San Francisco Examiner once pointed out, on TV the accountant was seen as a bland man in white tie and tails who handled the envelopes on the Academy Award programs. Or he was seen as a Donald Meek type of character in old movies and TV dramas. In the daily press the CPA was reported as the defendant in litigation alleging incompetence or even connivance with management, usually in connection with a failing company. Or, he was the subject of inquiry and investigation by a government legislative committee.

It is no wonder that the profession had a negative public image. Its attitudes were not known, its people were faceless, and its activities were mysterious. Indeed, in their broad public anonymity, accountants were sometimes referred to as the Gnomes of Wall Street.

Some members of the profession felt this did not matter, that since accountants were highly regarded by those they *directly* served, public opinion was not important and could be ignored with impunity—particularly since it was considered at variance with the facts (sic).

Importance of Public Opinion

Actually, every profession, every calling, must have public approval if it is to survive. History has shown the power of public opinion. And it is to be particularly reckoned with, in this day of all–pervasive communications, when the electronic and printed media can crystalize public attitude and incite action almost overnight.

What the public believes *is* important to accountancy. For the profession's publics include not only its clients in the business community, with whom it has direct contact, but also the millions of union members, investors, legislators, administrators, voters, judges—and even juries, all of whom can profoundly influence its future. Public understanding and approval can perpetuate organizations, institutions, and professions indefinitely. It can, for example, affect a profession's ability to attract talented young people. But public misunderstanding or disapproval, on the other hand, can destroy absolutely. The breaking up of the great American trusts in the early 1900s is a case in point.

In the increasingly volatile atmosphere of the late 1960s, the profession began to recognize that it must change the impressions of the past if it was to continue to move ahead in both private and public areas and make its traditional contributions to the economy. If not, its role would simply erode.

But after years of self–sufficiency in the circumspect handling of its own affairs, the profession was still reluctant to entrust its public image to public relations people—to professional communicators. They were thought prone to exaggeration and commercialization—something that went against the professional grain.

THE PROFESSION'S PUBLIC RELATIONS OFFENSIVE

Any reticence concerning the use of professional communicators quickly disappeared as firms were hit by the suits and indictments that were reported so prominently in the financial press. In the late 1960s and early 1970s firms engaged public relations people or press counselors—if they did not already have them. Almost invariably, they defended their positions and their people in statements carefully prepared by their lawyers and press counsel.

But these actions were defensive. At best they could only limit the damage to the firms' reputations. Therefore, more positive public relations exposures had to be undertaken at the same time.

The top partners of the various firms were introduced to the press through meetings and luncheons with editors and key writers for such prestigious publications as *Barron's,*

Forbes, Fortune, The Wall Street Journal, and *The New York Times.* They discussed their firms, the profession, and financial reporting with intelligence and candor. They submitted to questions and answered them freely. In so doing, they revealed themselves to the press as warm, sincere, and dedicated human beings—quite unlike the Gnomes they were thought to be. One particularly critical writer for *The New York Times* remarked on one of these occasions, "I wish you fellows had stopped in sooner—we would have had a little more to go on."

Efforts were stepped up to bring major talks by members of the profession to the attention of the press—particularly those relating to efforts of the Accounting Principles Board and the Financial Accounting Standards Board to improve financial reporting standards. Hundreds of copies of these speeches were supplied to prestigious colleges and universities for classroom use at both undergraduate and graduate levels. Members of the profession undertook more extensive works in the public sector at their own expense and brought these to the attention of the press through press releases and other pronouncements.

The accountants' reasoned views and wholesome attitudes began to be appreciated and discussed at important levels. By 1971, more constructive and positive press stories had begun to displace the negative ones. And by 1977, when the Metcalf Committee attacked the profession, some prominent business journals actually came to its defense.

Types of Press Releases and Publicity

Commercial enterprises traditionally bombard the press with annnouncements of new products or services, new locations, personnel changes, and similar developments, as well as with releases of financial information. Indeed, quarterly income reports of companies whose securities are traded in on the major exchanges appear regularly in *The New York Times* and *The Wall Street Journal.*

Generally, accounting firms have not sought similar

types of publicity concerning themselves or their practices. This has been deemed off limits under long prevailing ethics rules. Many new managing partners have been elected, locations added, mergers consummated, and even international firm names changed without formal notice to the press— although the information is sometimes conveyed less directly in other types of news stories, viz,

> In commenting on the New York financial debacle, Joseph Smith, the newly elected managing partner of the accounting firm of Aces and Clubs, noted today that . . ."

The release of information concerning numbers of staff, office locations, revenue figures or other financial data have also been expressly discouraged by ethics committees— although this is being relaxed as a result of the Metcalf Committee's recommendations. (See Chapter 9, The U.S. Profession)

A number of firms regularly furnish the press with information and observations concerning the technical substance of accounting; for example, developments in taxes or the quality of financial reporting in a particular industry— matters on which a professional accountant is qualified to speak. These ideas often originate in the firms' external publications and are brought to the attention of the press for whatever attention they merit. They are usually credited to the firm publication in which they have appeared. And, being largely informative and educational, these stories redound favorably upon the firm and the profession.

Accounting firms also call attention to books written by their members for possible review by the media and make the author available for interview. *Business Week* and *Forbes* sometimes publish such reviews and interviews with authors.

Occasionally a by–lined story extolling the global expansion of a particular firm or the accomplishments of its managing partner will appear in a prominent newspaper. These, no doubt, are suggested or at least encouraged by someone connected with the firm itself, and are considered a triumph from a purely public relations viewpoint. But they are usually an anathema to competing firms who feel they are equally deserving of such plaudits. And efforts to develop such stories have been long frowned upon by ethics committees.

Accounting firms, of course, are frequently mentioned favorably in the press without overt effort on their part, but simply as a result of their interface with clients. A story reporting the issuance of a qualified opinion on the financial statements of a publicly owned company is an example. It demonstrates the firm's objectivity and independence. The announcement of a change in auditors by a prominent company is also considered favorable to the newly appointed auditors—although unfavorable to the firm that has been deposed.

Although the profession's attitude against self–inspired publicity has mellowed somewhat over the past decade, it is likely to relax much more. At the time of this writing, accounting firms with publicly held clients are being pressed by legislative groups and government agencies to disclose important operating information and financial data. This no doubt will move the profession even further into the public arena. (See The Metcalf Committee's Recommendations in Chapter 9, The U. S. Profession.)

Caveats in Dealing with the Press. There are certain caveats that should be observed in dealing with the press. Among these, according to press counselor William Bostleman, are the following:

Do not ask to see a reporter's story before it goes to press. Such a request implies lack of faith in his ability and integrity. (Besides, he won't show it to you anyway—as a matter of policy). If there are technical points involved, the reporter will ordinarily check these with you, because he will want to be sure his story is accurate.

Do not ask the newspaper to send you clippings or tearsheets.

Do not thank reporters for "putting the story in." They would not use the story if it did not have news merit. What you *can* do is compliment the reporter on the way the story was handled or written.

Do not try to place publicity material in a newspaper by using influence with the business department.

Do not be offended if the editor or reporter does not write or cover the article the way you'd like.

Do not telephone a publication and ask why it did not publish your article. Chances are that you won't be successful with every attempt; however, in the long run, by adhering to accepted procedures, you will make friends among the members of the press, and your future relations will benefit.

Do not keep a writer waiting. He usually works on a deadline, and you will incur his disfavor as well as the antagonism of his editor if you waste his time. If it is imposssible to see him at once, get word to him so that he can decide whether he wants to wait.

CHAPTER 17

The New Client Proposal and Presentation

The obtaining of a new large audit client is the culmination of the entire marketing effort. It is the reward for developing and operating an effective organization dedicated to service. It reflects an awareness of all the factors and forces that bear upon the accounting profession and its publics and its markets—many of which are described in the preceding chapters. But it requires one final climactic drive—a vigorous proposal and presentation to the prospective client. This is touched upon briefly in Chapter 5, but is treated in greater depth here.

The Preliminaries

Most major companies that are about to change auditors invite proposals from several accounting firms. The U. S. Postal Service, for example, invited and received proposals from all the Big 8 Firms when it was engaging auditors in 1970.

Most proposals by large accounting firms to major companies involve a preliminary meeting, a survey, and a written proposal, followed by an oral presentation. The prospect then selects auditors from the competing firms, acting through a management or an audit committee, or even an entire board of directors. Far–flung enterprises usually want extensive information about each firm—office locations in the United States and abroad, the number of personnel, the types of services offered, the key clients served in each location and, of course, the estimated fee. These are often tabulated and evaluated by the prospect and compared one against the other with the idea of selecting the "finalists" and eliminating the others.

Whatever the form of the first contact or the size of the prospective client, alert accountants are quick to express enthusiastic interest in an engagement. In short order, they arrange a date for a preliminary meeting—that afternoon, the next day, or a few days later.

THE RESPONSE TO THE FIRST OVERTURE

The following type of response to a telephone inquiry from a prospective client is designed to convey the accountant's interest in the prospect and his company, and should start to instill confidence at the outset:

"Yes, we *are* interested, *very much* interested in talking with you about your auditing problems. We've had quite a lot of experience with money market funds and are familiar with most of the problems, including the valuation of portfolio securities. In fact, my partner, Bill Tansey, is working out a solution with the SEC right now. I'm sure we can help you—give you the type of service you need. Can we make an appointment to get together tomorrow or Friday? I'll have Bill join us."

In the brief interim between the first contact and the preliminary meeting, they collect available data on the prospect's industry, its business practices, markets, and competition, its tax peculiarities, and reporting aspects. They ascertain what clients they already have in the industry and the types of services they have performed for them. And they obtain the prospect's last annual report, if possible, and begin to match up their service locations with the company's apparent geographic needs.

They also endeavor to learn through *Who's Who* or other sources as much as they can about the prospect's people, their personalities and cultural backgrounds, where they live and where they went to school, their outside interests and affiliations, and who their friends are. If they are members of the audit committee of the prospect's board of directors, the accountants try to ascertain what existing clients they may be connected with.

The accountants' "proposal team" is usually comprised of people equal in stature and rank, and insofar as possible in background and interests, to their opposite numbers in the prospect's organization. They should be people who can sell the engagement—not boys sent to do a man's job. However, they take care not to overpower the prospect's representative or awe him to the point that he would believe the new auditors will have him fired for his deficiencies 6 months after they get the job.

Invariably, accountants will wish to demonstrate familiarity with a client's industry at the first meeting; if necessary, by importing an industry specialist from another location of the firm. A principal spokesman is designated to head the accountants' group and chair their presentation. Ideally, he should be an accountant of mature business judgment, articulate and skilled in piloting a meeting.

POINTING UP AN ASSOCIATE'S ACCOMPLISHMENTS

The chairman of the accountants' proposal team can often point up the qualifications and accomplishments of other members of the team more gracefully than they can themselves.

Accountants' Chairman: "Wes, as you may know, heads up our retail practice, firmwide. He also participates in the annual finance and accounting programs of the Retail Association: you may be familiar with his book *Curtailing Shoplifting Losses,* which is published by Empire Publishing. I believe you will find that Wes speaks your language and will offer you many helpful suggestions."

The term "preliminary" implies that other steps will follow. Generally, the preliminary meeting gives accountants an opportunity to ascertain the broad parameters of an engagement and to set timetables for an in–depth survey and written proposal. It also provides an opportunity to quickly impress the prospect with the depth of the accounting firm's talent in order to start building client confidence.

In some cases the proposal is successfully concluded at the preliminary meeting. This is more common with smaller companies, but it will occasionally occur with engagements of large companies as well. Firms sometimes gain large clients through a phone call followed by a meeting with company officers on the same day. Or, they may be notified by telephone that they have been selected as auditors by a Big Board–listed company that they did not know was changing auditors, let along considering their firm.

These are, of course, exceptions. In most instances the preliminary conference is simply the first step, to be followed by a survey, the preparation and filing of a written proposal, and finally an oral presentation.

Gaining Knowledge of the Prospect's Problems–The Survey

An on–site survey is the best way to gain an intimate understanding of a prospect's problems. And it can be critical if the accountants are to come up with a precise and competitive fee estimate.

The survey team generally includes audit, tax, and management consulting people. The company's operations and tax posture, as well as its accounting system, internal controls, and internal auditing function, is usually surveyed. And an effort is made to focus on detecting trouble areas or weaknesses that the accountants might help to resolve. Sometimes a limited operational controls review is made of some phase of the business to ascertain and quantify specific profit improvement opportunities. In sum, the survey equips the accountants to write and talk knowledgeably and convincingly about the company's audit and its problems and their approach to handling them.

ANTICIPATING THE PROSPECT'S PROBLEM

It is often possible to surmise the prospect's problem before the initial meeting with him. In that case, the accountant might elicit the client's interest and involve him in the presentation in somewhat the following manner:

Accountant: **"In looking over your income statement, we note that materials amount to 80% of your cost of goods sold. With the large investment in raw materials shown in the balance sheet and your low inventory turnover, we wonder whether inventories aren't a problem."**

Prospect: **"Yes, as a matter of fact, our raw material inventories are our biggest headache. We have so many types of items in there. Some turn over fast, and others stand still. Unfortunately, we haven't been able to determine which does what—and what the proper levels ought to be.**

Accountant: **"Well, there are techniques for determining this sort of thing. We have a computer program for analyzing inventories and separating them into fast, moderate, and slow–moving items. It's fairly simple and inexpensive to apply. With this type of analysis, you can establish appropriate base stock levels and economic order quantities with some confidence. And you can reduce your overall investment in inventories without interfering with customer service."**

The Written Proposal

The selection of auditors is rarely based solely on the information or data contained in a written proposal. Even major companies that endeavor to select auditors on the basis of comparative data furnished in written proposals and directories invariably make only tentative decisions at the proposal stage. They may *think* they have made their selection, but as a practical matter they often change their minds after they personally meet the people who will be responsible for the work.

Nevertheless, the written proposal should not be slighted. Instead, it should be regarded as an important, though not final, step in the proposal procedure. It should provide a solid factual background and completely exploit service possibilities.

The written proposal, of course, must be thought out more carefully than the oral presentation, since the latter can be modified on the spot in the light of observable client interests or response. The former cannot; once launched, it stands.

Ideally, the language should be active and conversational, not overly formal or stilted. The terms should be those of the prospect—not those of the accountants. The message should coincide with the prospect's expectations by focusing on his problems, and it should stimulate his involvement by discussing each problem specifically and intimately.

It must be recognized that the prospect is principally interested in the accountants' knowledge of the industry and representative clients as well as special engagements performed in the industry. The prospect is similarly interested in the personnel who will be assigned by the accounting firm to the engagement—their background and experience, and their solid accomplishments in dealing with problems similar to those of the company and others in the industry.

The prospect may also want to know about a firm's service locations, the general range of services offered, and representative clients *outside* his industry.

The prospect will ordinarily have only marginal interest in an accounting firm's history, organization, or training programs. This should be presented concisely—in no more than a paragraph or two. On the other hand, he may be extremely interested in the standing of the local practice office and its representative clients.

The length of a particular proposal is a matter of judgment. Usually, a smaller prospective engagement will call for a shorter proposal—perhaps a two–or three–page letter, accompanied by a firm publication with an article of particular interest. A larger engagement, on the other hand, might require a written proposal running up to as many as 25 or 30 pages. This must, however, begin with a brief summary letter highlighting the detailed data which follows.

A proposal should be only long enough to cover the relevant points concisely and completely–and no longer. All material must be pertinent and directed toward the prospect's situation and needs. If information concerning office locations or numbers of personnel is needed, for example, it should be "customized" by matching it with the prospect's geographic needs. A map or other graphic can be helpful here.

The writing must be consistent. The drafting should be assigned to the best writer, rather than to a "committee." While the writer should look to others for technical data, for example, to the audit, tax, or MAS people who "scoped" the engagement, he should be free to refine, restate, or even condense in his own style.

The Oral Presentation

This is probably the single most important stage in gaining a new client—particularly if there are a number of accounting firms competing for the engagement. It is essential that the momentum of the earlier efforts be maintained through this final phase.

Whether the accountants meet informally with a small group of officers or appear before the entire board of directors, their engagement team should be selected carefully, (see earlier discussion) with one partner designated as the chairman. He should, of course, be personable, articulate, and experienced in moving a discussion forward. He need not participate in the engagement, but if he intends not to, he should immediately give notice of the fact. All other personnel, however, should be members of the engagement team, fully prepared to make the necessary time commitments.

There are usually three stages in the presentation, all of which involve using the principles of communication.

Three Stages. The first is the "appraisal" stage, where the two principals and their lieutenants or subordinates size up one another. This interval of small talk can be as brief as a

---

RESPONDING TO A NAÏVE QUESTION

In fielding an uninformed query during an oral presentation, care should be taken to dignify the question and preserve the questioner's self respect. Here's a typical exchange:

Member of Prospect's Audit Committee—"I can't understand why we don't use American accounting in all our European subsidiaries."

Accountant—"I certainly agree that it would be highly desirable if the accounting in the foreign subsidiaries could follow American precepts. However, as you may know, accounting treatments are prescribed by law in many foreign countries, and there is no alternative but to follow them for local reporting purposes. Of course, the foreign statements are made to conform with our practices when they are brought over here and consolidated for U. S. reporting purposes. As a matter of fact, though, the American Institute of CPAs is working with professional accounting bodies abroad right now to get international accounting more uniform."

---

half minute—but should certainly never drag beyond several minutes. "Silent language" predominates here; personality and style set the tone. Ideally, the accountants decide, "We can do business with these people," and the prospects say to themselves, "They look pretty capable." On the other hand, the prospect may decide "these men are not for us." Or the accountants may turn off with the thought that "these guys are sharpies." If so, that's that, and everyone might just as well go home. Ordinarily, of course, the communication channels remain open, and the accountants go on to the second stage.

At this stage, the accountants begin to directly build confidence by launching into the prospect's problems and indicating how they will approach them. Two–way discussion should be encouraged by eliciting questions and comments from the prospect. The accountants must convince him that they have the technical competence, the intelligence, and the manpower to do the job. It is almost axiomatic that the prospect will manifest some "sales resistance" throughout this stage, since he does not want to be considered a push over. He will probably feel compelled to show that he is also knowledgeable; he may query or challenge some of the accountants' assumptions. The accountants must be especially sensitive to him; their answers must be straightforward, but moderate in tone. In short, they must give him the recognition he is seeking at this point.

Many questions may be asked during this stage. And they must be answered with a quiet assurance based on familiarity with the prospect's operations and his industry. Answers should be specific and deep.

References to the prospect's company and functions should be in his terms and in those of his industry. Above all, the accountants should convey the impression that they know what they are doing and have a precise plan, as well as a tentative schedule, for performing the engagement. They should know the personnel to be assigned, the starting and finishing dates, etc. Above all, they must firmly impress the client with their interest in him and in his operations.

DIPLOMATICALLY OVERCOMING OBJECTIONS

It is not realistic to expect to make a presentation without getting into some sort of controversy—or having the prospect enter some objections. This is the "cat and mouse" game we all play when we are interviewing salesmen. It is only necessary that the accountant enter into the spirit of this little game by giving pleasing answers. He should never "win" the argument or "*dis*agree," since he must win the prospect over to his side. Here are some examples:

Prospect's Objection—"You are handling my competitor's work."

Possible Response—"Yes, in fact we have many clients that are in your line of business. We find that companies generally tend to lean towards the accounting firm that handles their competitors' work. We have many motels among our clients, for example. Some of them are competitors of one another. But they came to us because they believed they would benefit from our specialized knowledge of the industry. And they do."

"Yes, we do serve some of your competitors. But we want you to know that our communications with clients are held inviolate and confidential. We do not discuss one client's affairs with another. You can rely on us."

Prospect's Objection—"Your fee seems high. I can engage the X Firm at half the price."

Possible Response—"Our fee is based on the standard hourly rates we find we must charge for the type of professionals we hire. As you may know, we go after the top ranking graduates and pay them commensurately. And we train them well—we have one of the most extensive training programs in the profession. This enables us to offer thoroughly qualified people, people who will serve you efficiently and effectively, people you can have confidence in."

When the substantive questions have been exhausted, there may be a short silence.

"ASKING" FOR THE ENGAGEMENT

Professional salesmen are taught to "ask" for the order directly and forthrightly at the end of a sales presentation. How does a professional accountant go about this appropriately? Here's a suggestion:

Accountant—"Mr. Prospect, we have enjoyed meeting with you and are impressed with your company and its growth. We want you to know that we would like to work with you and your people—we would be happy to serve you."

(Then wait in silence for the prospect's reaction—do not utter another word until he responds.)

The final decision may be "telegraphed" through a relatively innocuous question reflecting the last gasp of sales resistance. For example: "If your firm is selected as our auditors, when can you fellows start to work?" If the accountants can reply something like this—"We will begin work at all locations next Monday"—they have the engagement, and they should leave before the client changes his mind!

Index